PUFFIN BOOKS
ENVIRONMENTALLY YOURS

For thousands of years the Earth has given support to all forms of life – humans, animals, plants and insects. Now one of those species – the human species – is posing a massive threat to its well-being. People all over the world are suffering the effects of pollution, radiation and deforestation. Plants and animals are disappearing at a frightening rate and, worst of all, the Earth is heating up in a process called global warming.

But it need not be like this. There are plenty of people in the world who know enough to stop more damage being done and who can help save the Earth from destruction.

Environmentally Yours looks at just what *is* happening and what *will* happen if things carry on the way they are. Most importantly, it looks at what we can all do to help save the Earth and its inhabitants.

Early Times is an independent newspaper for young people launched in January 1988 with an estimated readership of 200,000. It regularly features articles on environmental issues and encourages its readers to think and act in a positive way to help save planet Earth.

GN00806334

EARLY 🌳 TIMES

The independent newspaper for young people

Environmentally Yours

A Green Handbook for Young People

Illustrated by Keith Brumpton
With cartoons by David Myers

PUFFIN BOOKS

PUFFIN BOOKS

Published by the Penguin Group
Penguin Books Ltd, 27 Wrights Lane, London W8 5TZ, England
Viking Penguin, a division of Penguin Books USA Inc.
375 Hudson Street, New York, New York 10014, USA
Penguin Books Australia Ltd, Ringwood, Victoria, Australia
Penguin Books Canada Ltd, 2801 John Street, Markham, Ontario, Canada L3R 1B4
Penguin Books (NZ) Ltd, 182–190 Wairau Road, Auckland 10, New Zealand

Penguin Books Ltd, Registered Offices: Harmondsworth, Middlesex, England

First published 1991
10 9 8 7 6 5 4 3 2

Text copyright © Complete Editions, 1991
Illustrations copyright © Keith Brumpton, 1991
Cartoons copyright © David Myers, 1991
All rights reserved

Early Times would like to acknowledge the assistance of Sandy Ransford and Diana
Vowles in the preparation of this book

Printed in England by Clays Ltd, St Ives plc
Filmset in 11/13 pt Sabon Monophoto

Contents

INTRODUCTION

It's a wonderful world we live in. Our planet works on a system of natural checks and balances where nothing goes to waste. Everything has a purpose and everything has a use.

The sun provides energy that heats the Earth and makes plants grow. Its heat makes the water in the rivers, lakes and seas evaporate and form the clouds in the sky. From the clouds comes rain to provide the water that is needed by all forms of life.

The animals on Earth breathe in oxygen and breathe out carbon dioxide. Plants breathe too. They make their food by a process called photosynthesis. This uses carbon dioxide, chlorophyll (the green substance in leaves) and sunlight. In this way they take in much of the carbon dioxide that the animals breathe out. The plants then release oxygen as their waste product, which is then breathed in by the animals.

Some animals are predators – they prey on other animals for food. If there were no predators, the herbivores (the animals that eat plants) would increase their numbers so much that they would starve through lack of food. And when animals die of diseases, their bones are picked clean by the carrion-eaters, such as crows, vultures and jackals. When they have had their feast, the insects and worms move in to finish the job. It's a neat way of making sure that rotting carcasses do not remain to spread disease.

So the Earth has a perfect system of give and take, of balance and proportion. Unfortunately, this balance of nature has been disturbed. Some environmentalists have been warning of this for many years – as long ago as 1896, Swedish scientist Svante Arrhenius predicted the effect that a doubling of carbon dioxide in the atmosphere would have on global temperatures.

Today the concern is much more widespread. Not a day goes by without an environmental, or 'green', issue being in the news. Often it's bad news – another rain forest destroyed, or a further increase of greenhouse gases. Sometimes it's good news – more cars using unleaded petrol, a new recycling scheme, or investments in windmills to provide clean, renewable energy.

The deterioration of the environment is a worldwide issue. It affects each and every one of us, no matter where we live, and to improve the situation will take a worldwide effort. But this effort need not – some say *would* not – come from governments alone. As individuals, we can have an impact on the future of our Earth.

Environmentally Yours looks at and explains the many problems that face us today: the greenhouse effect, the destruction of the ozone layer, acid rain, deforestation, toxic waste, endangered plant and animal life, the depletion of some of our energy resources. It explains how the methods we use in farming and industry, our transport and our everyday life, are contributing to these environmental dangers. Scientific forecasts are also given for the future if we simply continue as we are doing today.

If, as you read through the first few chapters, you begin to feel as if you are living on a doomed planet, read on. Chapter four reviews some of the many suggestions that have been made for steps that could be taken by governments and businesses to fight these environmental problems. Chapters five and six consider alternative energy sources and how we could transform our transport. And finally, there is a chapter aimed at you, the individual, filled with suggestions for practical ways in which you can help.

The issues of our environment – what's wrong, and what can be done – are the issues of a great debate. Many scientists believe that modern technology is the answer to all our problems. Many others question this, and say that we must adopt a new way of thinking about the Earth and our future on it. We must find a new and safer way of living to conserve our world for our children, grandchildren and great-grandchildren, for if we go on in the same old way, what sort of inheritance will we leave them?

Environmentally Yours gives you the facts and the forecasts, the problems and their possible solutions, that will enable you to join in this debate. Find out what's going on, and find out what you can do. Remember, it is *your* world.

Teach your children what we have taught our children: that the Earth is their mother. Whatever befalls the Earth befalls the sons of Earth. If men spit upon the ground, they spit upon themselves. The Earth does not belong to man, man belongs to the Earth.

Chief Seattle of the Squamish Indians in 1851

CHAPTER ONE

What's Wrong?

It seems that in some ways we human beings are just too clever for our own good. We have linked our natural inventiveness and creativity to our desire for progress, but the result may be that we are killing our planet.

The evidence of this is all around us. Many species of animals have been wiped off the face of the Earth, and we have lost many plants and insects that were never even properly recorded. We're living amidst the pollution of litter and waste we have created ourselves – fumes from car exhausts, throwaway packaging and an abundance of junk mail are just a few examples. This is more obvious if you live in a town, but things are just as bad in the country.

The country air, once clean and fresh, now may be carrying chemical pollutants from power stations and factories. The streams may look clear and sparkling, but many of them carry nitrates, pesticides and other chemicals down to the reservoirs that provide our drinking water. Some of our rivers and streams are now empty of fish, because they have all been killed by the poisonous brew. And in some rivers you can even see the thick foam caused by chemical wastes.

In the fields, the soil is full of poisonous chemicals that have been sprayed on crops to prevent disease and kill insects. These pesticides have killed birds, mice, foxes and badgers too. Many of the creatures that have survived the chemicals are struggling for existence as marshlands are drained, trees are felled and hedgerows are rooted up.

Go to the seaside and you can't fail to see the pollution

around you. Litter is scattered on the beaches. Some of it has been dropped that day by careless people and some has been brought in by the tide. Sewage floats in the water. The majority of Britain's beaches are considered by doctors to be a potential health hazard. And in the long hot summer of 1989, the clear waters off the Cornish coast were tainted by a slimy orange algae that few swimmers wanted to brave.

The various kinds of pollution and waste caused by the way we live today all contribute in different ways to our main environmental problems. And most of these problems are interconnected. For example, the destruction of forests does not just deprive animals and plants of their natural habitats: it also contributes to the greenhouse effect. In looking at these environmental problems one by one, remember that anything we do to improve things in one area often helps improve another area too.

• The greenhouse effect

The gases that exist naturally in the Earth's atmosphere let the sun's rays through to warm us, and they also trap some of the sun's heat, rather like the glass in a greenhouse does. If they did not, the Earth would be a frozen planet.

The problem we have to tackle is that the level of gases which trap the sun's heat is rapidly rising and the result is a kind of blanket in the air. The 'blanket' prevents an increasing amount of heat from escaping from the Earth's surface and so the global temperature is beginning to rise.

In the bleak days of a British winter, this may seem to be a good idea. In fact, it could be disastrous.

The cause of the greenhouse effect is the rise in concentration of the following gases:

Carbon dioxide: this is responsible for 50 per cent of the greenhouse effect. Its increase is caused by burning coal, oil and gas (fossil fuels), wood, and petrol in motor vehicles.

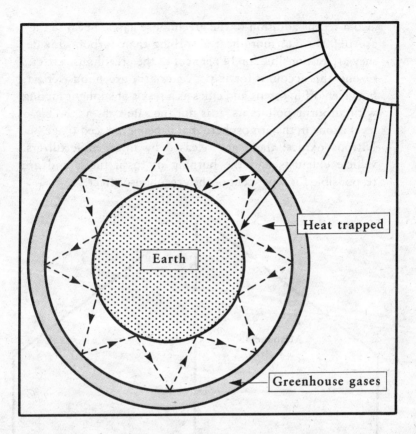

Its rise is being accelerated by the cutting down and burning of forests, especially the tropical rain forests.

Methane: this accounts for 18 per cent of the greenhouse effect and is thirty times more heat-absorbing than carbon dioxide. Its increase is due to people clearing forests and replacing them with cattle ranches and rice-growing paddy-fields. The flooded paddy-fields give off methane, and so does cattle manure.

Chlorofluorocarbons (CFCs): these are more commonly mentioned in relation to the ozone layer (see below), but are

also a recent addition to the greenhouse gases. Because they are 10,000 times more heat-absorbing than carbon dioxide, they are responsible for 14 per cent of the greenhouse effect.
Ozone: this accounts for 12 per cent of the greenhouse effect. It's given off in towns and cities as a result of sunlight mixing with airborne pollutants. It is not the same gas as the high-level ozone in the atmosphere that is being reduced (page 9).
Nitrous oxides: these are released by nitrogen fertilizers, vehicle exhausts and the burning of fossil fuels, and are responsible for 6 per cent of the greenhouse effect.

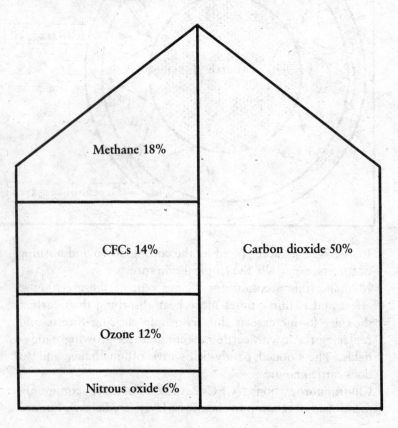

• The destruction of the ozone layer

Ozone is a gas that forms a layer in the upper atmosphere. It's a kind of oxygen that absorbs the ultra-violet radiation from the sun. It's these ultra-violet rays from the sun that burn our skin. Sunblock creams can screen out these burning rays, but they're not as effective as the ozone layer. Without it we wouldn't be able to go out at all unless we wore dark glasses and covered ourselves completely.

So when scientists discovered a hole in the ozone layer in 1987, it caused much alarm. The hole was over the Antarctic and it was as large as the United States and as deep as Mount Everest. Thinning in the ozone layer was later discovered in the Arctic too.

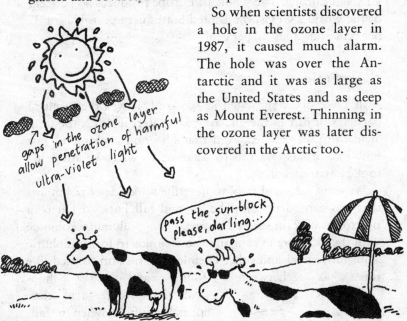

gaps in the ozone layer allow penetration of harmful ultra-violet light

pass the sun-block please, darling...

Chlorofluorocarbons

It's largely the use of chemicals called chlorofluorocarbons (CFCs) that's destroying the ozone layer. It may be hard to believe that by using hairspray you are affecting a gas thousands of miles away, but it is true. The CFCs contained

9

in most aerosols rise into the atmosphere. Their chlorine component combines with an oxygen atom from a molecule of ozone. This forms ordinary oxygen and chlorine monoxide, thus destroying the ozone. CFCs are also used in refrigerators and air-conditioning systems and in the manufacture of the lightweight packaging you see as hamburger containers and some egg cartons.

Britain is at present the biggest producer and exporter of CFCs in Europe. The whole of Europe produces 36 per cent of the world's CFCs, the United States is responsible for 37 per cent and Japan 12 per cent.

• Acid rain

In 1866, black snow fell in Scotland. It was the result of particles of dirt in the air. Six years later, in 1872, the term 'acid rain' was coined. And that's a good example of just how long it has taken us to wake up to what we are doing to the environment.

We now use 'acid rain' to describe all kinds of pollutants that are carried up into the air and fall back to Earth in the form of rain, snow or fog. The pollutants combine with the moisture in rain and snow clouds to form sulphuric acid, nitric acid and other chemicals. The rain formed like this is between four and a thousand times more acid than normal rainfall. When it falls to Earth it damages trees, lakes and streams, buildings and people.

The main chemical culprits that reach the atmosphere are sulphur dioxide and nitrogen oxides. Natural events such as forest fires and volcanic eruptions are responsible for a certain amount, but these chemicals are produced in much larger quantities by the burning of fossil fuels – gas, coal and oil.

Power stations produce much of the sulphur dioxide. They can be fitted with devices called flue-gas desulphurization systems to cut the amount of gas given off, but in Britain we have not yet done this. Power stations produce nitrogen oxides too, as do other industrial processes, and half of them come from vehicle exhausts.

• Deforestation

All over the world, the forests are disappearing. This is not just because of acid rain and other pollution. People are cutting the trees down to clear land for growing crops and keeping cattle. Sometimes they want the timber for building houses and making furniture. Sometimes they simply need it for fuel.

People have always cut down trees to use their wood. But in the past, there weren't so many people. Now the trees are being used faster than new trees can be grown. Forests the size of Belgium are destroyed every year in the less-developed countries of the world. In 1987 alone, Brazil lost 20 million acres of forest. Even if new trees are planted, a hardwood tree, for example, takes many years to mature.

Trees give off oxygen and absorb carbon dioxide – fewer trees mean less carbon dioxide is absorbed. The burning of trees to clear forests also releases more carbon dioxide into the atmosphere, increasing greenhouse gases. Deforestation has other effects as well. The tropical rain forests in central and South America, central Africa and south-east Asia are a particular cause for concern. Many species of animals and plants live in them, and if their natural habitats die, so will they. Many of our modern drugs have been developed from

11

plants found in the rain forest. Friends of the Earth estimate that as many as one quarter of our purchases from high-street chemists use substances that come from rain forest species. Many of the rain forest plants are being used in research for drugs to help the fight against cancer.

• The extinction of animal and plant species

It's estimated that at present we are destroying *100 species every day*. Among the animals that are facing extinction in various parts of the world are the Asiatic lion, the blue whale, the black rhinoceros, the elephant, the mountain gorilla, the tiger, the giant panda, the snow leopard, some species of crocodile, the peregrine falcon, the bird-winged butterfly – the list goes on and on.

In Britain we are in danger of losing the bat, several species of butterfly, the dormouse, the otter, the barn owl, the golden eagle, the nightingale and many plants. We have lost 95 per cent of our traditional hay meadows, and half of the rest are damaged. Some 99 per cent of lowland heaths have been built on, ploughed up or planted with conifers. We have filled in 90 per cent of our ponds and destroyed more than half of our wet marshy areas. Four-fifths of our limestone grasslands have gone.

In the last 50 years we have cleared 50 per cent of our lowland woodlands or planted them with conifers, creating conditions too dark for many plants and creatures to live in. This is more than was lost during the previous 500 years. And since 1947 we have destroyed 109,000 miles (175,381 kilometres) of hedgerow and four-fifths of our chalk downlands, which supported 30 different kinds of plants per square yard (square metre).

Not all of the precious resources were natural. Some of them were made by people hundreds of years ago. As they developed, they made homes for many different kinds of animals and plants. Many of these could not live in any other kind of habitat. Now that we are destroying these habitats, we are losing the creatures and plants that they supported, probably for ever.

• Fossil fuels

Coal, oil and gas are all fossil fuels. Like most of the energy on Earth, they were produced by the heat of the sun. Coal is the fossilized remains of large plants. Oil and gas are the fossilized remains of small plants and animals that lived on the Earth millions of years ago. But unlike other forms of natural energy, fossil fuels will not last for ever. Their supply is limited; once we have used them all up, we cannot replace them. The environmentalists' term for this kind of energy is 'non-renewable'.

Burning fossil fuels releases sulphur dioxide, nitrogen oxides, carbon dioxide, soot, ash and dust into the atmosphere. These pollutants contribute to the greenhouse effect and cause acid rain.

• Toxic waste

Toxic, or poisonous, waste is a by-product of many

13

industrial processes. Of the two billion tonnes of waste produced each year in Europe, 150 million tonnes is industrial waste. Of this industrial waste, 20 to 30 million tonnes are toxic.

People are becoming more and more worried about the toxic waste that industry produces. The facilities we have now can only dispose of 50 per cent of it.

In Britain we even import toxic waste from other countries for disposal. The reason that other countries want to send us their toxic waste to deal with is simple – we do it more cheaply. In West Germany, toxic-waste disposal costs £25 a tonne. In Holland it costs £15 a tonne. In Britain it costs a mere £5 a tonne.

From 1987 to 1988 we imported 183,000 tonnes of toxic waste and incinerated 100,000 tonnes of it in the North Sea. As it burnt, it released a deadly poison called dioxin, which can cause cancer in animals and affect their reproductive systems. Fortunately, this process will be banned from 1994.

Workers in many industries are more likely to develop cancer because of the materials they handle – for example, types of asbestos, dyes and, of course, anything radioactive.

It's not only the workers who suffer. People who live near toxic-waste dumps have a higher rate of illness. And sometimes the pollution reaches catastrophic levels through carelessness. In 1988 the water supply of Camelford, Cornwall, was polluted by 20 tonnes of aluminium sulphate. The lorry driver from the chemical company dumped it into the town's water supply instead of into the aluminium storage tank. Twenty thousand people suffered joint and muscle pains, headaches, vomiting, diarrhoea and blistering of the mouth. Some of them even saw their hair turn green. And 60,000 fish were killed.

• Population growth

In the late 1980s, the world's population topped the five billion mark – a 500 per cent increase in just 150 years. Today the population is growing at the rate of 150 people a minute. That's 9,000 per hour, 216,000 per day and 1,512,000 per week. Altogether, the population is increasing by a staggering 78,624,000 a year – that's just over a third of the population of the United States. It is estimated that, if we keep growing at our present rate, the world's population will level out towards the end of the twenty-first century at around 10 billion people – or twice as many people as today.

Most of this population explosion will take place in the less-developed countries of the world, but the industrialized nations – which currently use a far larger share of the Earth's resources – will also grow. More people will put more of a strain on the Earth's natural resources and habitats. The question is, can the Earth sustain it?

A bit of hair won't stay in place so you spray it back with hairspray.

An exhilarating lesson in the gym leaves you hot and sweaty. You cool down by spraying yourself with deodorant.

Each time this happens the hole in the ozone layer gets a little bigger.

I feel very strongly about the way we are ruining the ozone layer which protects us from the ultra-violet rays of the sun.

I wish people would take just a little time and trouble and instead of buying cans containing CFCs would look for an 'ozone-friendly' sticker.

Make an effort to stop the depletion of the ozone layer. It's YOUR environment as well.

Letter to Early Times *from Sarah Napuk, aged 13, from Edinburgh*

CHAPTER TWO
Some Causes

The problems we've just looked at can seem so over-whelming that it's hard to take them all in. But it's no good pretending they don't exist – they do. What's more, they are getting worse all the time. So how did we get ourselves into such a situation? Let's look at some of the contributing factors, one by one.

• Agriculture

Agriculture simply means farming – one of the oldest human activities. The practice of growing crops and manag-ing animals for food goes back thousands and thousands of years.

In the old days, farmers took the trouble to understand their land. They had to – if they didn't look after the soil, the crops were poor and they could not make a living. There were no easy answers, no bags of chemicals to help them out in the short term.

They knew that some crops took different nutrients from the soil than others, so they practised crop rotation. This meant that a field would one year be used for growing wheat, the next year it would grow turnips and the third year it would give grazing for cattle. In this way, the soil did not become exhausted.

Most farms were what are called 'mixed farms'. This means that the farmers grew some grain crops, such as wheat, barley or oats. They grew some vegetables, such as cabbages, turnips and beans. And they raised cattle, pigs, sheep and chickens for milk and meat.

They used some of the vegetables to provide feed for the animals in winter. They also cut hay in June, drying it in the sun before storing it in barns until it was needed for food. The straw that was left after they had harvested the grain was stored too. It made good bedding for the animals in winter. This straw, with the animal manure, was then spread on the land to give nutrients back to the soil. Nothing was thrown away and nothing was wasted.

Large trees were left standing in the fields. This was partly because they were hard to remove and partly because they provided shade for the animals in summer. Thick hedgerows were the best way of keeping the animals safely enclosed. They also made an excellent home for birds and small animals. These ate some of the seed, but they also ate the insects that would have eaten the crops. The farmers did not have chemicals to spray on the crops, so they had to rely on the 'balance of nature'.

It is this balance of nature that is destroyed by chemicals. Many insects are preyed upon by other insects, but the chemical poisons kill them all – 'good' insects and 'bad'. Then the birds and mammals starve or eat the poisoned insects and die out in their turn.

After the Second World War, the population of Britain increased, so farmers were expected to grow more food. At the same time, the chemical industries were discovering how to make 'agrichemicals', that is, pesticides, fungicides and fertilizers.

Some farmers began to realize that if they cleared away the hedges and trees, they could grow more crops per acre. The huge, prairie-like fields they created were much easier to spray with chemicals to kill pests and diseases. With no small fields left – they didn't keep animals – the new thinking was to specialize. To these farmers, the mixed farm was a thing of the past.

Without animals, there was no manure to fertilize the land. So the soil was fertilized with chemicals instead of organic material (manure and other natural waste products). These gave the soil the nutrients it needed but no bulk, so the soil became lighter and thinner. As there were no wind-breaks or deep-rooted plants to bind the soil, it was blown away by strong winds and washed away by heavy rain.

Nobody seemed to give much thought to the long-term effects of this kind of farming – or perhaps they just didn't care. For the type of person who farmed the land was changing too. The new farmers were business tycoons; profit was what they wanted. And the older farmers had to join in the race for productivity or be forced out of business by competitive prices.

Nowadays, more and more people are beginning to realize that there may have been some truth in what some people were saying all along – that you cannot farm in this way

19

ENVIRONMENTALLY YOURS

indefinitely. The land has been suffering from this treatment for years. Now our health is beginning to suffer too; we can no longer ignore the warning signals.

No less than 20,000 tonnes of pesticides are used every year on Britain's farmland. They are deadly poisons, and they are on the crops that we eat. Not only that, the rain washes them through the soil into the water-table and so into our drinking water. The nitrates that are used to fertilize the soil travel the same route, and it is possible that they may cause cancer.

The liquids that seep away from slurry (farmyard manure) and silage are polluting our waterways too. The slurry comes from the animals that are now housed in overcrowded conditions indoors. Silage is grass cut in May and compressed into fermenting bales to make winter feed.

Animal rights

Many people are now beginning to think more carefully about their food. They are becoming concerned about the amount of chemicals they might be eating at every meal. They have also begun to realize that food produced in the modern technological way simply doesn't taste very good.

The meat we eat today isn't like the meat of the past. Because people no longer want to eat fat, the animals are specially bred to carry little fat and more lean meat. They are fed on artificial foodstuffs and they are given hormones to make them grow, as well as antibiotics and other chemicals. Many are artificially bred too. For example, sheep are given hormones so that most of them give birth to twin lambs instead of just one. When we eat meat produced in this way, we take all these chemicals into our own bodies.

People are beginning to question, too, whether they want animals to be treated like this so that meat is cheaper to buy. Animals that are farmed intensively are not allowed to

20

live in a natural way and they suffer great stress as a result.

Pigs often spend their entire lives indoors in cramped conditions. As they have no fresh air or exercise, they are more likely to become ill. This means antibiotics have to be used to cure their illnesses, along with other chemicals to increase their weight. When the sows (female pigs) give birth, they are put in a special narrow pen with the piglets just outside. The piglets can reach the sow to feed on her milk, but the sow is kept a prisoner in case she rolls on the piglets and crushes them to death.

As for chickens, they are packed into tiny cages with wire floors. Their wings and beaks are clipped so that they cannot attempt to fly or peck each other. They are often fed on their own waste and the remains of other chickens. With no exercise or healthy food, their meat has less taste. And because some of the chicken waste they eat is infected with salmonella, the disease can spread throughout the whole flock.

However, some people claim chickens kept in this way are healthier. A spokeswoman for the National Farmers' Union has said that hens kept in battery cages are less diseased. This is partly because they do not stand in their own droppings and partly because they don't pick up so many parasites. The idea is that because they are kept under shelter with carefully controlled temperature and lighting, they should actually be healthier than free-range chickens. And because of the huge scale on which they can be farmed and because the eggs are easier to collect, poultry and eggs are cheaper to buy.

Many people think that the way farm animals are managed today is quite wrong. They are kept in unnatural and uncomfortable conditions, then sent crammed together in lorries to slaughterhouses where they are killed. Sometimes they travel long distances without food or water.

Taking into account all these facts, many people have decided to become vegetarians. Linda McCartney, for example, thinks that killing any animal for food is wrong. 'I don't believe in murdering animals,' she says. 'When you're eating a spare rib it's not a "spare" rib, it's an animal's rib. It's not beef, it's a dead cow. If abattoirs had glass walls, people would be vegetarian.'

Other people think that if the farm animals are allowed a natural life, it is all right to eat meat. It is possible to buy meat that has come from animals that were not treated with chemicals, were allowed to wander freely outdoors and were humanely slaughtered. However, such meat is expensive and some people feel that the farmers' duty is to produce food that everyone can afford, not just wealthier people. In this way, they justify the suffering of the animals.

So what can we do if we don't want to support intensive farming, but can't afford free-range meat and eggs? The simple answer is that we can eat less meat. We don't need it to be healthy – in fact, nutritionists say that too much meat is bad for us. We can eat more vegetarian food and, when we do eat meat and eggs, we can make sure that they have been produced as humanely as possible.

• Industry

Until the middle of the eighteenth century, Britain was an agricultural nation. There was some industry, but it was on a small scale. It existed mainly to meet the needs of the local people. For example, the people who made furniture, wagons, clothing and shoes were skilled craftsmen who sold their goods to their neighbours.

The Industrial Revolution

From 1760 onwards, there was a great change in the way people lived. Machines were invented that could make things much faster than the old craftsmen did. The people left their homes and small workshops to go to the big new factories. Gradually the machines drew the population from the countryside into the towns to find work. This process became known as the Industrial Revolution.

As the people flocked into the towns, the towns grew into large, dirty, industrial cities. People lived in overcrowded and unhealthy conditions. The water was often polluted, there were no proper drains or sewers, and the air was filled with smoke.

The smoke came partly from the fires that were all the people had to keep themselves warm and partly from the factory chimneys. The factories belched out other fumes as well as smoke, adding to the health hazards of living in the city. With the smoke came soot. This fell from the air and left a black layer over everything.

23

This kind of pollution continued until the Clean Air Acts of 1956 and 1968 stopped most of it. We seem to live in better conditions these days, but is industry really any cleaner?

Industrial pollution

Industry produces a massive amount of pollution, much of it in the form of toxic waste materials. It also produces enormous amounts of carbon dioxide, which is adding to the greenhouse effect. The countries of Eastern Europe alone are thought to contribute 25 per cent of the total carbon dioxide output of the whole world. Factory chimneys pour out chemicals that cause acid rain. The pollution from the factories and power stations in Britain has fallen in the form of acid rain as far away as Sweden, and many lakes there are now 'dead' – unable to support living organisms – as a result.

Then there's the problem of the CFCs that are destroying the ozone layer; companies make aerosols for us to use for everything from polishing the car to killing the cat's fleas.

(Many manufacturers are now employing alternative methods to aerosol, so always read the product label first – choose those that say 'Pump action' or 'Produced without the use of CFCs', or simply 'Ozone friendly'.) Most importantly, CFCs are also used in refrigerators. In the West, we can afford to look for alternative, perhaps more expensive ways of making our refrigerators work. In the developing countries, where a refrigerator is still a modern luxury and the climate is often much hotter than ours, things are different. The Chinese are planning to make 300 million refrigerators using CFCs.

Many industries are thoughtlessly destroying the rain forests. For example, the tropical hardwood trees of southeast Asia are cut down to supply the Japanese market. In Japan this wood is used for things as ordinary as concrete shuttering – that is, the frame that holds concrete until it sets. It is then thrown away. In this country tropical hardwoods are used carelessly too. We should not destroy the world's rain forests to make windowframes and lavatory seats when pine, a quick-growing tree, would do the job just as well.

There are many other ways in which industry and business are throwing away our world. Have you noticed the amount of mail that comes through the letter-box each morning? Most of these heaps of mail are unwanted letters from companies trying to sell you something. They buy people's  names and addresses from other companies or from the local councils. They then send out thousands and thousands of letters to people who have never heard of them and probably do not want to know about them. People groan, 'More junk mail', and then throw the letters in the dustbin. But letters are made of paper, which means that trees have been cut down. They have been delivered, which means that petrol and oil have been used. And when they are thrown away, they add to the piles of waste that must be got rid of.

Finally, industry demands huge amounts of power in the form of our non-renewable fuels – coal, oil and gas.

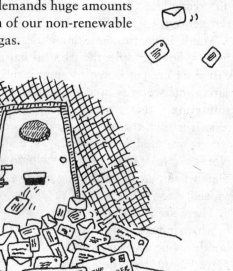

• Energy

Almost all energy on Earth comes from the sun. Even the fossil fuels were produced originally by the heat of the sun. Unlike these non-renewable fuels, the sun's energy is limitless. It might sometimes seem as if the sun doesn't come out very much. Yet if we could learn to trap all the sunlight that falls on Earth in just one hour, we would have enough energy to supply the whole world with fuel for a year.

So far, scientists have not discovered any way of doing this. We must still get our energy from burning fossil fuels and wood. We can harness the rivers to make hydroelectricity, and of course we can use direct solar power – that is, the sun's heat. We can use the power of the wind and the tides and the heat that is locked deep in the Earth – geothermal power. In the less-developed countries, people use animal power. And, of course, we have discovered nuclear power.

Each person in the Western world uses a quantity of energy each year that is equivalent to burning 6 tonnes of coal. Where is this incredible amount of energy going to come from as populations increase and fuel reserves decrease?

Solar power, wind power, tidal power and the power from living creatures are renewable resources. As long as the sun and Earth exist, the sun will provide heat, the tides will ebb and flow and the winds will blow. An ox or a donkey that pulls a cart or works a water-pump can be replaced by another animal when it grows old. And if we plant fast-growing trees and do not use them more quickly than we can grow more, we won't run out of wood to use for fuel.

As we've already seen, coal, oil and gas are non-renewable resources. So is nuclear fuel. Strictly speaking, geothermal power is non-renewable too, but we usually think of it as a renewable source because it seems to be limitless. Most of our energy comes from non-renewable resources:

Oil	40%
Coal	30.3%
Natural gas	19.6%
Hydroelectricity	6.7%
Nuclear fuels	3.9%

The non-renewable fuels that account for almost 90 per cent of our fuel-use are not simply pollutants; they are hazardous in other ways as well.

Coal-mining, particularly open-cast mining, destroys the landscape. It creates ugly and dangerous tips that look like small mountains. In 1966 one of these tips slid on to a school in Aberfan, south Wales, killing 116 children and 28 adults. Coal-miners suffer from lung disease because they breathe in coal dust every day at work.

An oil spillage spells catastrophe for the environment. The huge oil tankers sometimes collide or run aground and their oil then leaks into the sea. The worst disaster to date was in 1989, when the *Exxon Valdez* leaked 11 million gallons of oil off Alaska. This created an oil slick measuring 1,000 square miles (2,590 square kilometres) and 2 million gallons of oil was washed on to the beaches. Thousands of birds and animals died, including peregrine falcons and bald eagles, which are both endangered species.

Supporters of nuclear power say that it is a clean fuel. This is because it does not produce fuel by burning and so cause pollution. Instead, it releases energy by the splitting of the nuclei of atoms of elements such as uranium.

Mrs Thatcher has said in the House of Commons: 'Nuclear power does not produce greenhouse gases and therefore reduces global warming.' British Nuclear Fuels, who control nuclear power in Great Britain, spend thousands of pounds on advertising to tell us the same thing. This is in part due to the public being so alarmed by the Chernobyl accident in Russia in 1986. After this incident, Peter Vey, the director of public affairs for the Central Electricity Generating Board, said, 'A growth in adverse public opinion could halt the nuclear programme ... We urgently need a campaign to educate and reassure the public.'

In spite of this campaign, most people *are* worried by nuclear power. In fact, 70 per cent of the population are against it. It's very expensive to produce, and very inefficient. Worst of all, its effects are highly dangerous and very long-lasting.

Nuclear fuel gives off radioactive radiation. In a high enough dose, this kills people immediately. Smaller doses that build up over a number of years cause cancer. The fuel gives off radiation for thousands of years after it has been used, and we simply don't know how to dispose of it safely.

Nuclear fuel is due to run out in only 60 years. Closing down nuclear power stations and trying to dispose of their contents will be very expensive. And the most frightening thing is that if the fission process – the splitting of the atomic nuclei – got out of control, the nuclear power station would explode. This would cause loss of life and environmental catastrophe on a scale we can hardly imagine.

When the Chernobyl reactor overheated, it gave off clouds of radioactive gas and dust. All animals and plants in the area close to the reactor died. A cloud of gas drifted over

29

Europe, killing thousands of migrating birds. As the cloud passed over Britain a few days after the accident, heavy rain in the hilly districts of Wales, Cumbria and Scotland brought radioactive dust with it. Cows and sheep that ate the grass were affected by radiation, and their milk and meat was declared unfit for human consumption.

Four years after the accident, 400,000 acres (162,880 hectares) of British farmland was still radioactive. 1,200 miles (1,930 kilometres) away, in Chernobyl, the trees and plants near the site have strange, unnatural forms and nobody is able to live there.

In San Francisco the earthquake of 1989 has made the Americans realize how dangerous nuclear power is. Luckily, none of California's nuclear plants was in the danger zone. Michael Mariotte, director of the Nuclear Information Research Service, said the nuclear plants could not have withstood the quake. 'In a shut-down plant in Sacramento, fuel rods are being removed from the radioactive core,' he said. 'If an earthquake had knocked one rod loose, it would have been a real disaster.'

Where should the waste go?

There is a lot of argument about nuclear waste. No one wants it near them, but it has to go somewhere. Even Dr Edward D. David, science adviser to the former American president, Richard Nixon, admits, 'One feels queasy about something which has to stay underground and be pretty well sealed off for 25,000 years before it is harmless.'

It's a huge problem. The figures on the possible dumping of nuclear waste at Dounreay, Scotland, give an idea of its scale. The dump would cost £1.6 million. It would cover 350 to 400 acres (142 to 162 hectares) underground and 200 acres (81 hectares) on the surface. That's the size of 190 football pitches below ground and 100 above. There would need to be 26 caverns 820 feet (250 metres) square. These would be 1,500 feet (457 metres) underground. For safety, the nuclear waste would have to be stored for thousands of years. But Britain is only a small island. How many of these nuclear dumps would we have room for?

Some nuclear waste has been released into the Irish Sea. Many people are concerned about this. The Department of the Environment says that plutonium from the Sellafield plant in Cumbria is polluting the Solway coast of Scotland. Greenpeace, the environmental organization, says that 85 per cent of the radioactive plutonium discharged from Sellafield is trapped in coastal sediments. These are stirred up by storms and blown as sea-spray inland. There they settle as dangerous dust in people's homes.

The children who live near Sellafield are ten times more likely to develop leukaemia (a kind of cancer of the blood) than the average child in Britain. Child leukaemia is also

Fast reactors yea or nay?
Pretty hard for me to say,
When the experts put their case
It seems to me their tails they chase.
All I do is hope and pray
Mankind will not have to pay!

31

high in areas surrounding other nuclear plants. Yet British Nuclear Fuels says there is no proof that radioactivity is the cause.

Although nuclear fuel is now expensive, John Collier, chairman of the Atomic Energy Authority, says that fast reactors are the answer for the future because they are more efficient. But Peter Roche of the Scottish Campaign to Resist Atomic Menace (SCRAM) says, 'The European collaboration on fast reactors has disintegrated. The French fast reactor at Superphenix hardly works, the Germans are unable to open theirs at Kalkar because of political opposition, and the Italians have pulled out because we have withdrawn funding.'

In July 1989, more than 100 top British scientists, including two Nobel prize-winners, signed their names to an advertising campaign. This warned that concentrating on nuclear power will worsen global warming because people will neglect to tackle its causes. The money used for developing nuclear power would be better spent combating global warming. For example, the scientists calculated that using energy more efficiently would be seven times more effective in cutting the production of carbon dioxide than the use of nuclear power.

So wouldn't it seem sensible to develop safer, cleaner forms of energy? But in 1986 Britain spent just £14 million on researching new forms of energy. In the same year we spent £300 million on nuclear power. Nicholas Ridley, a former Environment Secretary, called 'green' solutions 'vapid romanticism'. He said they called for 'a massively expensive programme of environmental measures without any justification, let alone any acknowledgement, of the costs and the effect those costs would have on people's incomes and the national economy.' In other words, he thought that trying to find 'green' solutions to the energy problems was idealistic, too expensive and simply not practical.

Wasting energy

In Britain we are very wasteful with energy. In the oil crisis of the 1970s, petrol supplies were running low. People in the Western world were told to save fuel by not making unnecessary car journeys and by driving more slowly. We were encouraged to turn the heat down in our homes. Yet in 1989, Cecil Parkinson, who was then Energy Secretary, said that 'market forces' must decide how big a part Britain would play in fighting the greenhouse effect. He said that the people of Britain could not be forced to save power. But if we can save fuel when there is a crisis, surely we can save it all the time so that there is no crisis in the future?

As our power stations produce electricity, they lose more heat than is gained from North Sea gas every year. This heat could be saved and used to heat homes. It is in Denmark – 32 per cent of home heating comes from Combined Heat and Power Stations (CHP) or from District Heating. District Heating is a system in which one central source heats many buildings, often from burning rubbish. In Britain just 3 per cent of home heating is produced in this way.

Our houses, too, waste energy. They are often badly insulated and very draughty, so they are expensive to heat. Some time ago, experimental houses were built in Salford and Milton Keynes to see how much energy could be saved. The people who lived in them spent only a quarter as much money on heating them, yet they were warm and cosy. But builders did not follow this example. The Building Regulations, which give rules on how buildings are constructed, were not changed to save energy in new houses.

Woodruff T. Sullivan III, Professor of Astronomy at the

University of Washington in Seattle, America, produced a fascinating example of the way we use energy as if it were unlimited. He put together photographs of the Earth at night that had been taken by satellites. All the world's cities could be seen lit up. Housing developments along America's main highways and the Trans-Siberian railway across Russia could be seen. So could Japan's fishing fleet, which uses light to attract the fish. In contrast, most of China, Africa and South America were lost in darkness. His photographs showed clearly how a quarter of the world's population uses three-quarters of its electricity.

• Transport

Out of all the energy we use in Britain, 20 per cent is used in transport. Nowadays that mostly means road transport, which is the most inefficient, polluting and wasteful use of resources there is.

Road transport uses 85 per cent of the European Community's transport energy. It carries 61 per cent of freight traffic and 84 per cent of passengers. Railways use only 3 per cent of the EC's transport energy to carry 23 per cent of the freight and 9 per cent of the passengers. Aeroplanes take 10 per cent of the energy and carry 7 per cent of the passengers and only a small amount of freight. The following diagram shows this starkly. It shows that to carry the same number of passengers, cars use over twice as much energy as trains and planes use five times as much. This is why conservationists want rail transport to be developed.

Only about 15 per cent of the energy in a car's petrol actually moves it. The rest is wasted. And apart from the waste, there's the massive pollution cars cause. They give off carbon dioxide, nitrogen oxides and carbon monoxide, all of which contribute to the greenhouse effect. Carbon monoxide in high concentrations is a deadly poison, too, and nitrogen oxides cause acid rain. Over half the nitrogen oxides in the air are created by oil-burning transport. In Britain there are now 20 million cars, producing a total of 800,000 tonnes of nitrogen oxides every year.

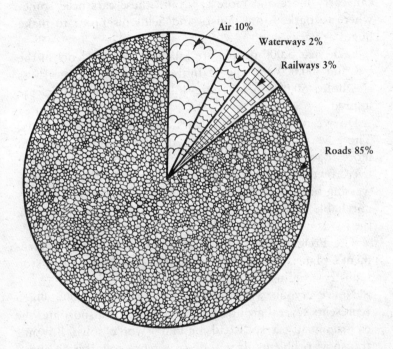

Air 10%

Waterways 2%

Railways 3%

Roads 85%

Cars also give off hydrocarbons, which irritate people's lungs and may cause lung disease. In addition, cars that use leaded petrol produce lead pollution. Over two million people in the European Community are affected by lead poisoning. In Los Angeles, 50 per cent of the city is taken up by roads and parking spaces. Surprise, surprise – LA is well known for its high level of smog (air pollution).

All in all, there's not much good that can be said about

road transport. And it's not only the pollution it causes that is destroying our environment.

Cars and lorries need roads – ever-wider roads, and more and more of them. Houses are knocked down and countryside destroyed in the rush to provide them. The motorways can carry more and more cars, and these cars need somewhere to park. More houses and fields disappear to make huge car-parks.

Each year 5,000 people are killed in car accidents in the UK and 300,000 are injured. In the European Community as a whole, 50,000 people are killed and 1.5 million are injured.

Do we really want more cars and lorries on the roads? The government thinks we do. In 1989 it announced that more roads would be built and more widened. It said that overcrowding on the roads was damaging the economy, wasting time, delaying deliveries and making manufacturers unreliable. The economic benefits gained from improving the roads would be twice the cost of constructing them.

The Freight Transport Association said of the government's plans: 'We are delighted. It is literally going to stop industry grinding to a halt.'

Not everyone was so pleased. Transport 2000, which represents several groups concerned about transport and the environment, says, 'Road building won't solve Britain's transport problems. It will destroy more countryside and it will add to pollution.' Stephen Joseph, the director of Transport 2000, points out: 'It has been estimated that just parking all the new cars forecast by the government (that is, a doubling of cars in Britain in the next forty years) will need an area larger than Berkshire. If they all moved at once they would fill a road from London to Edinburgh 257 lanes wide. We have a choice between protecting our environment and doing something to combat the greenhouse effect or creating more road space for more and more cars.'

Jeremy Vanke, the transport expert of Friends of the Earth, has said: 'The environmental consequences of the plan will be disastrous, both in terms of destruction of the countryside, homes and communities caused by construction, and the inevitable increases in vehicle emissions and energy use which will result from increased traffic.'

Building new roads does not in fact stop traffic jams. For proof of this, just look what happened when the M25 was built. It forms a ring round the outskirts of London, and the people who wanted it built thought it would be the answer to many of the city's transport problems. Much beautiful countryside was destroyed to make way for it. Yet already

it needs widening, because there are so many cars and lorries using it that traffic jams now occur every day. If the conservationists are right, the extra lane that is to be built will simply fill up with yet more cars.

It is estimated that traffic congestion costs nearly £15 billion a year – and it costs every household in the overcrowded south-east of England £5 a week. So why do people want to travel by car?

What's wrong with public transport?

One answer could be that public transport is unreliable.

You might wait a long time for a bus. As you wait, you know that the longer the bus takes to arrive, the more likely it is to be full. In London the tube trains are often crammed full to bursting. Sometimes even the stations are so full they have to be closed. The trains and stations can be dirty and unpleasant. There are not many staff to be seen, and some people are afraid to travel at night for fear of being attacked.

Rail transport is more reliable than it used to be. Yet it is expensive. A long-distance journey by coach costs less than half the train fare. If more than one person is travelling, it's much cheaper to travel by car. And in spite of the cost of the ticket, commuters travelling to London in the rush hour think they are lucky if they get a seat because the trains are so full.

In most country areas you simply can't manage without a car. In the past, country bus services were usually infrequent, and many people lived miles from the bus route. As more and more people could afford cars, fewer people used the buses. The bus services were cut because they were losing money. There are now so few bus services that nearly everyone needs a car to get to the shops, to school and to the doctor. People who cannot afford a car have to rely on the kindness of their neighbours.

As for the trains, most of the branch-line railways were axed in the 1960s by Dr Beeching, then Chairman of the British Railways Board. Trains now only go to the large towns and people need a car to get to the station.

As for planes, many of them fly half-empty. They use enormous amounts of fuel, and there are more and more in the sky every year. They make lots of noise and they sometimes have to dump their fuel in mid-air, which falls hazardously to the ground, causing more pollution.

Transport is a huge environmental problem. To beat it,

we need better and cheaper public transport. It must run on less wasteful and less polluting fuel systems. To achieve this we need proper transport planning (see Chapter six).

• Consumerism

Consumerism simply means buying – the goods we buy and how we buy them. The pattern of consumerism in this country has changed a lot in the last 20 years.

People used to go to several shops to buy their daily goods. They went to a butcher to buy meat, a fishmonger to buy fish and a greengrocer to buy vegetables, which were often grown locally. Canned food, sugar and so on came from a grocer. Toothpaste, cosmetics and medicines meant a visit to the chemist.

In the food shops, the goods would be weighed on scales and put into a paper bag. Sometimes they were tipped straight into the shopping-bag. Meat, fish and bread would be wrapped in special paper.

These days, people usually do their shopping in a supermarket. There they can buy all the goods they want under one roof. Nearly everything is pre-packed. All the fruit is the same size and colour and it looks very attractive. But it looks this way because it has been treated with insecticides, hormones and other chemicals. A Cox apple grown in Kent, for example, has been sprayed twelve times with growth regulators and insecticides while still on the tree. After picking, it has been sprayed with fungicide to make it store well. People are now beginning to wonder if they want to risk eating all these chemicals just so that the fruit looks nice and lasts longer.

The packaging the supermarkets use is another problem that is beginning to worry people. It uses up our precious resources. The paper comes from trees and the polythene from oil, and we just throw it away. Frequently the check-out person will put something that is already packaged into yet another plastic bag. If this happens with something you are buying, say that you don't want the extra bag – and if there isn't a long queue behind you, explain why not.

The plastic waste produced in Britain each year works out to 126 pounds (57 kilograms) for each person. Our dustbins overflow with bottles, cartons, polythene bags and Clingfilm. Altogether, plastics make up 20 per cent of British rubbish.

Disposing of all this plastic is an expensive problem. But that's not all. Making the plastic uses up energy and causes pollution, adding to the greenhouse effect.

Unfortunately, some of this packaging doesn't reach the dustbins. It becomes litter instead. Some people simply tear the wrapping off sweets and throw it away. They drop their cigarette packets and cans of drink without a thought.

In the town, this litter looks horrible. But at least someone will eventually clear it away. In the country, it remains in the fields and on the roadsides unless the people who live near by pick it up. In the mean time, it can kill or injure farm animals. Bottles and cans cause cuts, and the animals may eat polythene bags and die, or put their heads in them and suffocate.

It is an offence to drop litter. If you see someone doing it, you have the right to report them to the police.

Consumer demand

We want to buy things that look nice. But as we have seen, the glossy, uniform-sized fruit that we like to buy may endanger our health. For a long time, advertising has told us that 'whiter than white' means clean and hygienic. But do we really need babies' disposable nappies to be sparkling white? These nappies have been bleached using chemicals containing dioxins. In large doses, dioxins are highly poisonous. They are getting into the environment and building into harmful concentrations, and what about baby's bottom?

As yet, we don't know what the safe levels for dioxins are, but the Environmental Protection Agency in the USA suggests that they should be handled with the same care as plutonium, which is radioactive. So we know that 'whiter than white' does not always mean clean and healthy. Sometimes it means just plain dangerous. Fortunately, several manufacturers have realized that some people don't want their babies' nappies to be sparkling white – not if it means the baby will grow up in a polluted world. These manufacturers have begun to bleach nappies in a safer way.

It's not just nappies that are disposable in our world. The new consumerism has taught us simply to throw away things we don't like. In the old days, people would 'make do and mend'. Goods would be repaired, painted, darned, altered, lengthened, shortened – anything to make them usable again.

41

Today people have more money. Labour is more expensive, so it can cost more to get a radio or hairdrier repaired than it does to buy a new one that has been made in a less-developed country where labour is cheap. Whereas at one time people's homes would look much the same for their whole lifetime, there is now fashion for 'interiors', just as there is for clothes.

When people move house they often decide they don't like the previous owners' taste. They throw kitchen and bedroom fittings, baths and basins on to a skip for disposal. Then they refit their houses, often with tropical hardwood products. When the next person comes to buy the house, the same thing happens all over again. More of the tropical rain forest has been destroyed just to be wasted.

Our habit of buying things that look nice without counting the environmental cost doesn't stop there. It allows the trade in fur and ivory to continue. Some people don't seem to mind if animal species become extinct. They only think of what they want to wear.

In Africa the elephant is in danger of becoming extinct.

Although in some African countries killing elephants is restricted or banned, poachers go right on killing them. They are paid to do so by people who know that this ivory is illegal. It is passed from trader to trader and the price goes up each time. Finally it is made into jewellery and trinkets for people to buy. Because some of the ivory is legal, and because no one can tell the difference, it can be sold in any shop.

Each year, there are fewer and fewer elephants in Africa. But we can't lay the blame on the poachers. Many of them are poor people trying to earn money to feed their children. They don't even get paid very much by the traders. In the end, the blame lies with the person who buys the ivory. If no one wanted to buy it, the elephants wouldn't be killed. It's as simple as that.

If you see your friends buying or wearing ivory, explain this to them. Ask them if they really want elephants to vanish from the face of the Earth so that they can have a piece of jewellery. Once they have thought about it, they will probably see things your way.

This all points to one thing. We must learn to re-think the way in which we buy. In fact, we must learn to think *before* we buy. We must ask ourselves what our purchase means to the environment. Manufacturers spend thousands of pounds on advertising to encourage us to buy, throw away and replace with new – it keeps the cash registers ringing. Unfortunately, it also keeps pollution rising and resources dwindling.

• The causes of the problems

We've looked at some of the particular causes of some of the problems. But there are a few general causes from which all the problems arise.

In the West, we have come to accept the idea of always looking for more growth, always making more improvement. By 'improvement', many people mean more goods and more luxuries – not improvement to the environment which, in turn, deteriorates.

In the less-developed countries many people have a very poor standard of living. It is natural for them to want improvement, because for them 'improvement' means clean drinking water, a solid house and enough food to eat. Most of all, it means education for their children, so that they may have easier and healthier lives.

It makes our 'improvement' look pretty selfish, doesn't it? To keep striving ahead is part of human nature. It's how we explored the world, learnt how to fly and even went to the moon. But there comes a time when we have to ask ourselves whether our throw-away, buy-new society makes sense. Might it not be better to make things last longer in exchange for living in a better environment?

Having children is natural. In some agricultural societies, having many sons means there is more labour to farm the land. There are no state benefits, so the parents must rely on their children to support them when they are old. In the poorer societies many children die young, so people don't expect all the members of their large families to survive to adulthood.

But because of the improvements in medical care in this century, the world's population has grown explosively. The bigger population requires more food, more energy and more space. As more and more land is cleared, more animal populations are threatened. More resources are used and more pollution is caused.

In the 'developed' countries the population growth has slowed down. People no longer feel they need to have large families. But now some people are beginning to worry that

Britain will shortly be a nation of old-age pensioners. They don't see that a smaller population will put less pressure on the Earth.

And this is the third general cause of our problems – we are too often so busy thinking about the near future we don't worry about the long term. Governments and the public alike are reluctant to look far ahead. People can't quite believe that catastrophe may happen in their lifetime. But if we don't mend our ways very soon, there may be no way of stopping it.

When God made the world I don't think he should have made us. In the River Thames a thousand fish have died because of pollution and fishing and being selfish. The sea is so dirty we can't swim in it in places. If we don't stop being selfish the Earth will come to an end.

Sent to Early Times *by Christopher Ennals, aged 7, from Hampton in Middlesex*

CHAPTER THREE

A Bleak Future?

We've looked at what we're doing wrong and how we are destroying our planet. We've seen that the way we have been living has given us plenty to worry about. The main problems we face are:

the greenhouse effect
the destruction of the ozone layer
acid rain, and the destruction it causes
deforestation
the extinction of many animal and plant species
the depletion of our energy resources.

It's a list that makes grim reading, you'll agree. So what will happen if we don't try to solve these problems?

No one can be absolutely sure. They are problems we have never encountered before and the position changes all the time. But scientists have made predictions and they are alarming.

• The greenhouse effect

According to scientists, the increase in greenhouse gases will cause an average rise in temperature of 2 °C by the year 2050. This will vary from 1 °C at the Equator to 5 ° or 6 °C at the North and South Poles. The Earth has already become 0.5 °C warmer in the last ten years.

This might not sound very serious. But during the last Ice Age (which ended about 10,000 years ago), average temperatures were only 4 °C lower than today. Those 4 degrees meant that 30 per cent of the land area of the world was covered in ice. Today only 10 per cent is covered. This gives you an idea of just how much difference a few degrees can make.

If the Earth's temperature does increase by 2 °C, the polar ice-caps will melt. In turn the sea level will rise. In fact, the sea has already risen 4 inches (10 centimetres) since the beginning of this century. But scientists predict that in the next 50 years the sea will rise between 8 inches (20 centimetres) and 5.5 feet (1.65 metres).

It's not hard to see what the results of this rise would be. Indeed, in some parts of the world we can see the effects already.

Low-lying land would flood. This means that people would be left homeless and their crops would be killed by the salt water. In the Carteret Islands, near Papua New Guinea, some people have already had to leave their homes because the sea water is washing around their houses. In Redcliffe, near Brisbane, Australia, the sea is expected to rise by 31 inches (80 centimetres) by 2030; some people have just abandoned their homes because no one wants to buy them. And some islands, such as the Maldives in the Indian Ocean, would disappear completely beneath the sea.

In Britain we would not escape. London would flood, and so would some parts of the south and east coast. Some people believe that a huge part of eastern England, including all the Fenlands, would be under water. So, too, would the land near to estuaries like the Severn, the Humber and the Tees.

One fifth of the Earth's surface is covered by permafrost. This is a layer of soil that is permanently frozen, and in some places it's many feet deep. Because of global warming, it's starting to melt in some parts of Alaska. This means that houses are starting to sink, roads are breaking up and lamp-posts are leaning at crazy angles.

Some parts of the permafrost would be bog if they thawed out. The bogs would release massive amounts of methane into the atmosphere. The methane would increase the greenhouse gases, the Earth would become warmer still

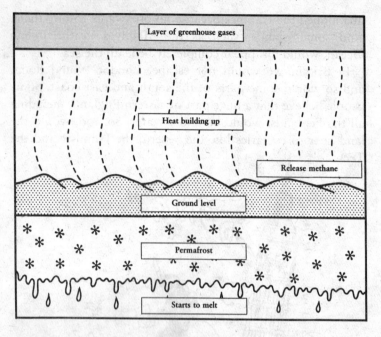

and more ice would melt. We would be trapped in a vicious circle.

Global warming will change the patterns of the weather world-wide. Hot, dry areas will become hotter and drier. Wet and stormy areas will get wetter and stormier. This will mean that growing food will become difficult. In Thailand it has already become too dry to grow rice in some parts of the country. To the Thai people, rice is a traditional crop and it is a main part of their diet.

The Ugandans depend on their coffee crop to bring money into the country. A temperature rise of 2 °C would mean that they could not grow it, and that would mean the economy would be ruined. The less-developed countries, whose population is doubling every 30 years, cannot afford to lose their crops.

Global warming could spell catastrophe for wildlife. The polar bear, which lives on the polar ice-cap, could lose its habitat and die out. The crocodile, which produces only male young in hotter weather, could die out too because there would be no females to breed. And in many countries, where the animals are already under pressure because their habitat is being destroyed by agriculture, things could get even worse. With ever more people to feed, and more land needed to allow for the failure of crops, the animals wouldn't stand a chance.

• The destruction of the ozone layer

As we have seen, the destruction of the ozone layer means less efficient filtering of the sun's ultra-violet rays – which contributes to global warming, as well as increasing the risk of skin cancer.

When it was discovered in 1987, the hole in the ozone

layer over Antarctica created so much concern that 46 countries agreed to halve the use of CFCs by 1999. This meant that the amount of chlorine in the upper atmosphere would still be four times the present level by 2010. In June 1990 a general world-wide agreement was reached to ban CFCs by the year 2000 – but this still means it will take years to reduce the chlorine in the upper atmosphere to its 1987 level.

Some people think it's already too late to save the ozone layer. Other people say that if we ban CFCs and other ozone-destroying chemicals immediately, we may still be in time. But at the time of writing, it's still not possible to buy a refrigerator that does not use any CFCs. (Some manufacturers do claim that their refrigerators have only half as many CFCs as other makes, so if your family is about to buy one, make sure you check on this.)

There's no argument about one thing: all the scientists agree that as the ozone layer is destroyed, more and more radiation from the sun will reach us. It won't only burn our skins. It will increase the cases of skin cancer and of eye cataracts. It will make us less resistant to disease and parasites. It will cause skin and eye problems in animals too, and even fish and other creatures living in clear water will be affected. And it will cause poor harvests world-wide.

• Acid rain

Acid rain has caused much damage in Europe and the United States. In the States, forests in Vermont are dying because of the pollution from the power stations in Ohio, 1,000 miles (1,610 kilometres) away. The trees in Europe are dying too – 64 per cent of them in Britain and 50 per cent in West Germany. Czechoslovakia, Greece, Sweden, Belgium and Holland are also badly affected.

In southern Norway, nearly all the lakes and streams are dead, that is, no animals or plants can live in them because they are too acid. The acid rain has dissolved metals and other pollutants and washed them into the water. It washes metals into drinking water, too, and this can cause serious illness. In Sweden, people's hair has even turned green because of the amount of copper in their water supply.

In Greece the Parthenon is crumbling. It has stood for over 2,000 years, but it cannot withstand the corrosive action of acid rain. Nor can the Taj Mahal in India nor St Paul's Cathedral in London. Many buildings, and even railway lines, are being destroyed by acid rain.

Fortunately, there is some good news. Something is being done to halt the damage, although progress is slow.

A law was passed in the United States in 1981 that all cars must be fitted with catalytic converters. These filter out a lot of the nitrogen oxides, as well as carbon monoxide and hydrocarbons, and can reduce the pollution from cars by up to 70 per cent. They can only be fitted to cars that run on unleaded petrol. The European Community has agreed that catalytic converters will be fitted to all new small cars from 1992.

President Bush announced in June 1989 that the US production of acid rain will be reduced by more than half in the next ten years. As from 1995, cars built in the US must run on non-petrol fuels such as ethanol and gasohol (see page 86).

The first flue-gas desulphurization system in Britain will be fitted at the Drax power station in 1993–4; this will reduce the emission of sulphur dioxide. There are plans to build natural-gas-fired power stations at a number of sites in northern England and Wales. These will give off less carbon dioxide and nitrogen oxide and no sulphur dioxide at all.

Environmental groups say that a lot more needs to be done before the Earth will benefit from these measures. But at least we have made a start in the right direction.

• Deforestation

Twenty-one years ago, forests covered a quarter of the Earth's land area. Today they cover only a fifth. It's predicted that by the year 2000 they will cover a sixth, and by 2020 just a seventh. The tropical rain forests are a special cause for worry; these unique habitats took 100 million years to develop and yet it's taken just 40 years to destroy half of them. And if we don't take drastic action *now*, they will be gone completely within another 40 years.

This would be a tragedy – not only because we would

have lost a remarkable and beautiful feature of our world. The burning of these rain forests is thought to release up to 25 per cent of all carbon dioxide into the atmosphere, so continuing destruction will make a large contribution to greenhouse gases. Deforestation destroys topsoil, leaving large areas of land much less fertile and more liable to flooding. We would lose access to many of the chemical compounds being used in drugs and medical research. Rain forest destruction could also have other ecological effects, such as changing weather patterns.

• Endangered species

We've already looked at a list of some of our animal species that face extinction, and have seen how pollution and deforestation can destroy natural habitats for plants and animals. Trade and population growth play their part as well.

A number of animal species have, of course, become extinct over the centuries, but one half of all known extinctions have occurred in just the last 100 years. If we continue at this rate, it's thought that we could lose a further one million species in the next decade. The same principles apply to plant life: at least 60,000 species of rain forest plants are in danger of dying out for ever in the next ten years if deforestation continues at its present rate.

• The energy trap

It's the industrial countries that use most of the world's fuel. For example, the average person in Britain uses 300 times more energy than the average person in the Himalayan country of Nepal. As industrialization continues to increase, and world populations continue to grow, the demand for energy will grow too. The Central Electricity Generating Board has estimated that the demand for electricity in Britain alone could increase by 20 per cent in the next ten years.

No one can be absolutely certain, but scientists predict that the non-renewable fuels we currently use for our energy needs will, at current levels, run out within the following time spans:

Oil:	in about 50 years
Natural gas:	in about 50 years
Coal:	in about 300 years
Nuclear fuel:	in about 60 years

As supplies diminish, prices will rise. And as we burn away our fossil fuel resources, we will continue to add to the pollution of our environment.

The world needs a friend
To love and depend on
In times of trouble . . .
The world has hope yet
If we children let it
And if we do it right
Together we can make the world
A better place
Because the world's best friend
Is you!

Sent to Early Times *by Miriam Mackley, aged 10, from Welling in Kent*

CHAPTER FOUR

Towards a Better World

It's clear that the destruction of the environment is not just a British problem. We alone are not totally responsible. Nor will we alone suffer the consequences. Global warming and the depletion of the ozone layer do not have national boundaries. The poisoning of the land, the destruction of wildlife and its habitat and the pollution of the seas are universal.

Together with other industrialized countries, Britain is responsible for the hole in the ozone layer over the Antarctic. The acid rain from British power stations is poisoning lakes and rivers in Scandinavia. If the Brazilians keep on cutting down and burning vast areas of the Amazonian rain forest,

the great AMAZON CHAINSAW MASSACRE

'WHIRR'

cert. X.

the climate in Britain will get hotter as the greenhouse effect accelerates. For once, the people of the world share a common enemy. The destruction of the environment will affect everyone. The thinning of the ozone layer will not discriminate between the rich banker in New York, the farmer in China and the schoolchild in London. The enemy that we have created must be fought world-wide by us all.

So what can we all do to save and improve our world? There are many things that you, as individuals, can do – and that you can start doing right now (see Chapter seven). But environmentalists believe that governments and businesses must act too. Through international co-operation, new laws and financial incentives, governments can act to protect the Earth rather than destroy it. Industry can invest in research and development of new processes and technologies that reduce pollution, lessen waste and use natural, renewable resources.

Lots of ideas have been put forward by organizations such as Friends of the Earth, Greenpeace, the Green Party, the World Wide Fund for Nature, Transport 2000, the World Health Organization and many more. The suggestions in this chapter are just some of the actions that have been recommended. Lots of people agree with some of these ideas, and some people agree with all of them. Today there are few people who disagree with all of them. One thing is clear: most of these environmental alternatives have a cost. It's not cheap to replace all our power stations, or to build public-transport systems that serve a growing population efficiently and economically. Doing nothing, however, could eventually cost the Earth.

Read through these suggestions and see which of them you agree with. Which ones come top of your list? And how realistic do you think they are?

• Agriculture

1. Grants and subsidies could be provided by governments to encourage a gradual change to organic farming. This means farming without artificial fertilizers and chemical pesticides; pesticides that are non-toxic could still be used.

Farms that use today's 'conventional' methods are often given financial assistance by the government. The Soil Association, among others, wants the same sort of assistance made available to farmers who want to convert to organic methods, which costs money and means smaller crops. The groups who are promoting this change in emphasis believe that up to 20 per cent of Britain's farming could be organic by the end of the 1990s.

With organic farming, the soil would be enriched with animal manure and 'green' manure (plants that give nutrients to the soil). It would take some time before the poisons drained away from our soil and water, but eventually they would be clean again. The reason the land would produce smaller harvests is that the crops would be attacked by pests. As the balance of nature was restored, the natural predators would keep the pests down. Our animals, birds, wild flowers and butterflies would start to thrive again.

2. All food animals could be bred, reared and slaughtered more humanely. Farms that manage livestock could be given money to move from 'factory' farming to more organic methods. The Soil Association has set out standards that it believes are necessary to ensure that our meat is safe and our livestock well treated. These include:
- forbidding prolonged confinement or tethering of animals
- ensuring that all livestock has access to outdoor pastures during the grazing season

- managing the size of flocks and herds to avoid animals feeling either loneliness or stress
- ensuring that organically grown food forms the major part of the livestock diet
- forbidding most additives and all unnecessary drugs.

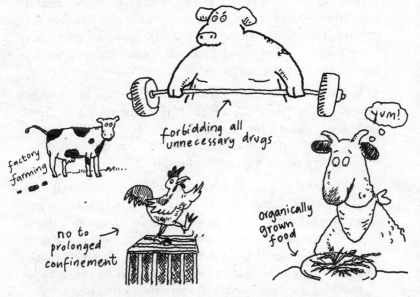

factory farming

forbidding all unnecessary drugs

no to prolonged confinement

organically grown food

yum!

3. Landowners could be paid to look after their resources. The government could give grants to encourage them to save wetlands, woodlands and sites of special scientific interest (SSSIs).

• Industry

In 1987, an international report on the environment called *Our Common Future* pointed out that, world-wide, seven times more goods were being manufactured in the late 1980s than in 1950. One of the report's recommendations was to

61

try to develop systems of production that respected the preservation of the Earth's ecological balance. How can industries achieve this? Most environmentalists agree that it will take the combined pressure of consumer power and government legislation to ensure that industry really does begin to clean up its act. At the moment, UK environmental legislation – and its enforcement – is fairly thin on the ground. Here are some of the many suggestions that have been made for laws and financial incentives that would make industry more 'green':

1. Industrial polluters could be taxed. A range of environmental proposals put before Parliament in early 1990 included a carbon tax: power stations and factories would pay a specific new tax related to the amount of carbon dioxide they released into the atmosphere.

2. The reduction in sulphur dioxide emission could be speeded up by fitting more flue-gas desulphurization equipment in power stations. This would mean a huge investment – it's estimated that the current programme could cost £600 million – but would bring Britain more in line with reductions in sulphur dioxide emission promised by other European countries. Less sulphur dioxide means less acid rain.

3. Restrictions could be put on the amount of toxic waste imported into Britain for disposal. The industrial production of toxic wastes could also be severely limited. Those industries that have no other way of making their product could be given government grants to develop new ways of manufacturing.

4. Grants and taxes could be used to make sure industries produced as little other waste as possible. And they could burn what waste they did have to produce energy.

5. Friends of the Earth wants energy efficiency standards for

electrical goods and a requirement to label these goods to tell the consumer how much energy they consume. This already happens in the United States.

6. Packaging laws could be introduced to encourage the use of re-usable glass rather than plastic. In Denmark it's illegal to sell drinks in non-refillable containers. West Germany limits the production of non-refillable drinks containers – and taxes the plastic containers that are produced.

Manufacturers and retailers could also be encouraged to reduce the amount of packaging they use. We need good packaging to protect and preserve products, and to provide consumers with information about what they are buying – but keeping it to a minimum uses fewer resources and reduces waste.

7. Industries and businesses that are environmentally conscious could be given tax concessions. This would encourage other companies to follow their example.

• Energy

We *must* save energy. We've already seen how carbon dioxide levels – and therefore greenhouse gases – will rise if we continue to use fuel at our current rate. But if we can *reduce* the amount of energy we use, some scientists think we could reduce the level of carbon dioxide by between 18 and 23 per cent by the year 2005. Chapter five looks in some detail at alternative, renewable sources of energy. But what could be done to reduce the amount of fuels we use now?

1. There could be regulations to make sure all buildings were properly insulated, and grants could be given to help people pay to insulate their homes. The Centre for Alternative Technology estimates that on average we lose 75 per cent of our heat. It simply goes outdoors – through the roof

63

(20 per cent), the walls (25 per cent), the windows, floors and under doors (30 per cent). Loft and wall insulation, double or secondary glazing and draught-stripping would all help capture more of this heat. New buildings could have solar panels to help with their heating.

Regulations made in 1990 mean that new buildings will save up to 20 per cent on energy – which will save 100 tonnes of carbon dioxide from being put into the atmosphere – but more could still be done.

2. Restrictions could be put on the amount of lights used by shops and businesses at night after they've closed. A certain amount of light is needed for security reasons, but much of the bright lighting in shop-windows at night is just for advertising. Flashing neon signs for advertising could be banned.

3. Businesses and homes that did not use more than a certain amount of energy could be given financial rewards (apart from lower bills!). During the oil crisis in the 1970s, there were regulations to keep the heating down in public buildings.

4. Programmes could be introduced to promote energy efficiency. Friends of the Earth has estimated that the use of electricity – which supplies 15 per cent of our energy demand – could be cut by up to 70 per cent through efficiency measures.

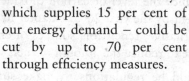

capturing industry's waste energy for use in the home

These include:

- capturing wasted heat from power stations for use in nearby factories, homes and offices
- improving the energy efficiency of electrical appliances
- replacing the light bulbs we commonly use with new fluorescent lights that last five times as long and use 80 per cent less power.

• Transport

In Chapter six we'll look in some detail at long-term changes that could be made to reduce energy consumption in transport. However, there are other ideas that could be started very soon, and so reduce the damage that vehicle exhausts are doing to the environment.

1. The government has already provided a big incentive to people to switch to unleaded petrol, by taxing it at a lower rate than leaded petrol. Yet by the end of 1989, only 35 per cent of motorists who could use unleaded fuel were doing so. According to the Campaign for Lead-Free Air (CLEAR), this was due mainly to motorists' confusion about whether or not they could switch to unleaded. Most modern cars will run on unleaded petrol after a simple adjustment to the engine timing. Special discs can be put in the petrol tank, enabling the vehicle to run on unleaded petrol. Continuing government-funded campaigns would be an effective way to get the unleaded message across to more people.

2. A similar campaign could be launched to tell people about the benefits of catalytic converters (page 54). Fitting catalytic converters to cars can be expensive; some countries offer a tax incentive to help cover the cost.

3. Tax incentives could also be offered for fuel efficiency. Smaller cars that use less petrol would pay less road tax than larger ones. This would be measured by engine size, and could apply to lorries and vans as well.

4. Tax advantages for company cars could be abolished. At the moment, many companies give their senior employees a car to drive because it means they don't have to pay so much tax. This encourages even more people to use cars.

5. Companies could be given financial incentives to send their freight by rail or water rather than road.

• Consumerism

1. If people really care about the environment, they can use their consumer power to help save it. A survey has shown that over a quarter of shoppers would be willing to pay at least 20 per cent more for goods that don't harm the environment. More and more people want to buy these goods. In the long run, manufacturers would be forced to provide only safe products, because most people wouldn't want to buy ones that were unsafe.

2. If people refused to buy goods that have too much packaging, manufacturers would have to rethink their ways. A good example of wasted resources is a carbon ribbon for an electric typewriter. The ribbon comes in a cardboard box. Inside this is a plastic bag. Inside the bag is the plastic cassette, and just a tiny bit of it is taken up by the ribbon. The ribbon is the only bit that is used – all the rest is thrown away. This is a waste of precious resources and it adds to the waste problem.

3. Everything that can be recycled should be. Recycling reduces waste and helps save energy. Making 'new' glass

from recycled glass uses 25 per cent less energy than starting from scratch. In Switzerland 55 per cent of glass is recycled; in Britain it's just 15 per cent.

In the United States the councils provide dustbins that are divided into compartments for plastics, glass, newspapers and so on. This could be done here. Bottle banks are springing up everywhere, but at the time of writing we still have only one bottle bank for every 16,000 people. In Holland there's one for every 1,400 people. And we need many more facilities to recycle paper, plastic, aluminium and steel. Some cities, such as Sheffield in South Yorkshire, are at the forefront of this movement and have special recycling centres, but many others are lagging behind. You'll find out more about recycling in Chapter seven.

4. Some people already invest their money to help the environment and this idea could be made more popular. The way it works is that people put their money into special investment trusts. These trusts only invest this money in companies that don't risk harming the environment. For

67

example, they couldn't invest in companies that are responsible for nuclear power. Instead, they would invest in a company which made solar panels. This encourages the growth of 'green' companies.

• Wildlife and natural habitats

1. Rain forests could be managed rather than destroyed. At an international conference on air pollution held in Toronto, Canada in 1988, one of the main recommendations for immediate action was to halt deforestation and increase afforestation. Environmentalists know that forestry management can work. In 1984 the World Wide Fund for Nature (WWF) sent a team of experts to Sri Lanka to look at ways of saving the Sinharaja rain forest from further destruction. As a result of the WWF action plan, more than 500 potentially endangered plant species have been saved, and local

people now earn money by making furniture and baskets from the palm trees that grow in the forest. WWF is currently working in African forests in Cameroon and Nigeria.

In 1989 Britain signed an agreement with Brazil to give advice on how to reduce rain forest devastation. It was the first time Brazil had ever signed such an agreement with a Western government.

2. There is already an international agreement to regulate and protect trade in wild animals and plants. Called the CITES (Convention on International Trade in Endangered Species) treaty, it has 102 signatories – but is proving difficult to enforce. Our government, and others, could speak out for stricter enforcement. Some conservationists, and governments, think that there should be a complete ban on trades that endanger wild animals – for example, trades in fur, ivory and rhino horns. Other people believe that some legal, controlled hunting of species such as elephants is a good thing, because limited trade would provide money to look after herds and protect them from illegal poachers.

3. Great whales are currently protected by law though some great whales continue to be killed for alleged scientific purposes. However, no such regulations exist to protect the related species of dolphins and porpoises; conservationists think that they should.

• Other improvements

1. We must save Antarctica from development. It is the last great wilderness left on Earth. Several countries are interested in it, partly for its minerals and partly because they want military bases there.

Australia and France have both refused to sign an

agreement to allow mining there. If they continue to refuse, Antarctica could become a protected area, or 'world park' as Greenpeace suggests.

2. We could try to find ecological solutions to ecological problems. Here's a good example: in New Mexico, the US government is using camels to eat undesirable plants on scrubland. This means they have not had to burn them, or use bulldozers or weedkillers. This kind of ecological problem-solving could be applied much more widely.

3. People could put more thought into how the Earth is exploited for profit instead of going for the obvious solution. For example, scientists have calculated that the Peruvian rain forest could yield more wealth than the land would if cleared for cattle or timber. The figures are:

Income for 1 hectare (2.5 acres/10,000 square metres)	
For fruit and rubber (preserving the forest)	£4,400
For cattle (destroying the forest for ever)	£1,910
For timber (destroying the forest for ever)	£2,055

Scientists have also done calculations about money gained from oil and fishing in Alaska. The Arctic oil reserve is thought to be worth about $64 billion. Fishing is worth $1.8 billion each year. As long as the fishing is properly managed, in 35 years it will produce as much revenue as the oil – and it will continue to produce revenue for the foreseeable future. The oil will run out in about 50 years, and if it is not carefully managed in the mean time, it will destroy the fishing. Some American experts think it might even run out within the next 12 years.

4. We must find a safe way of disposing of our sewage. At the moment, our seas and some of our rivers are heavily polluted with it. All sewage should be treated. The waste could then be used as fertilizer, or dried and burnt to provide power. It could also produce methane that could be a source of power.

Of course it's impossible for all these things to happen overnight. Yet we must try to start putting them into practice to change our world from one that is heading for disaster into one that is sustainable, and has a long future. If enough people have the will, they can force governments to act. And once governments begin to act, then we can all look forward to a better future.

If the nuclear power stations and the chemical weapons continue to be used the world will be destroyed. Just think of the Chernobyl disaster. A nuclear power plant exploded and here in Britain, on the other side of Europe, people were not allowed to eat fresh fruit or vegetables from their garden.

In the North Sea seals are dying because the fish they are eating are polluted. If the human race is not careful, we will die like the seals.

Sent to Early Times *by James Cullen, aged 11, of Sedbergh in Cumbria*

CHAPTER FIVE

Alternative Energy Sources

Within the next hundred years or so, we will have to find energy from alternative sources. This is because the fossil fuels will all have been used up, apart from coal. Of course, we also need alternative sources so that we can put a stop to pollution. Unless there is some amazing new discovery, these alternative sources of energy will be the renewable resources described in this chapter.

Renewable resources can provide different sources of energy, such as heat, movement and electricity. They can be produced near to the areas where they are needed, so that no energy is wasted in transporting or transmitting them. Most of them produce little or no pollution, and they will never run out.

Let's take a detailed look at these resources and their advantages and disadvantages.

• Solar power

The sun is the ultimate source of all energy on Earth. Even in our cloudy country, it could provide a hundred times more energy than we need if we could harness it. It's silent, clean and renewable. At the moment, it's only used in a very small way for heating buildings and water. An even smaller capacity is used for generating electricity.

The chief disadvantage of solar power is that its supply varies according to the weather and the season – and, of course, it's only available in the daytime. This means that it

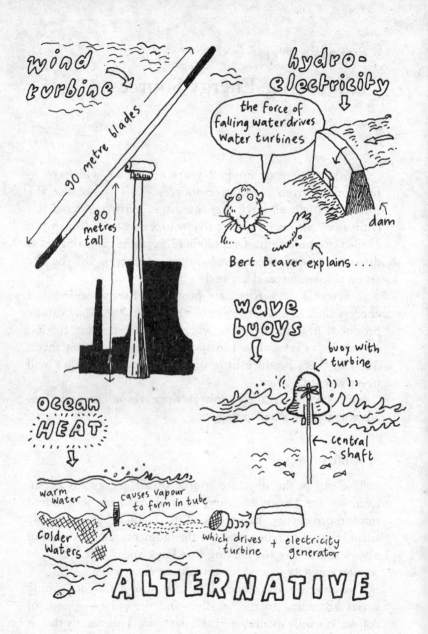

wind
turbine

90 metre blades

80 metres tall

hydro-electricity

the force of falling water drives water turbines

dam

Bert Beaver explains...

wave buoys

buoy with turbine

central shaft

Ocean HEAT

warm water

causes vapour to form in tube

Colder Waters

which drives turbine

+ electricity generator

ALTERNATIVE

74

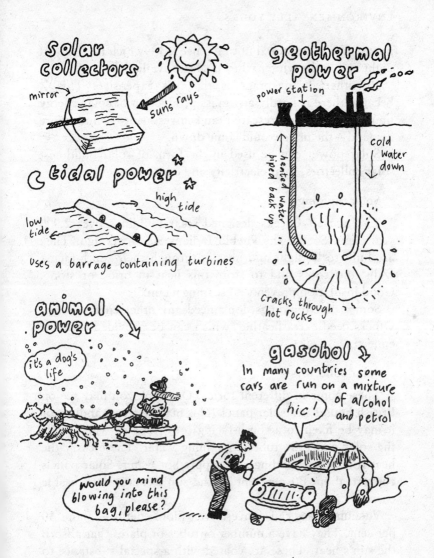

ENERGY SOURCES

mostly has to be stored until it's needed – which is chiefly at night and in the winter when it's least available!

Its other disadvantage is that it's expensive. This is because there is hardly any mass production of solar-energy units. With more research and investment – and more demand – the price would come down.

Solar power can be used in the form of solar buildings, solar collectors, solar electricity and ocean heat.

Solar buildings·

The ancient Greeks designed solar buildings over 2,000 years ago. So did the Pueblo Indians 900 years ago. They are built to let light and heat in through their south-facing walls and roofs and to store this heat in brick or stone. Good insulation prevents it escaping again.

Some solar buildings don't need any other energy at all. Others need extra heating, which can be provided by solar collectors.

Solar collectors

These come in different forms. One type you may see on British houses is a solar panel. This may be free-standing, or it may be fixed to a south-facing roof-slope or wall. Inside the solar panel are tubes containing water. These carry the heat round the building and supply hot water. Solar panels convert about 30 per cent of the sun's energy into usable energy.

Vacuum tubes can convert even more energy – about 50 per cent. They have a number of tubes or plates that absorb the sun's heat. These are coated with a special substance to stop the heat escaping. The tubes are in a plastic or glass cover from which the air has been removed to stop heat-loss by conduction or convection. They are another way of heating buildings and water.

Solar ponds

These lakes of salty water are used in Israel and the United States. One example is the Dead Sea, which produces electricity. When the sun heats the surface of the lake the hotter, denser layers of salty water sink, while the colder, lighter layers rise. The hot water can be stored at the bottom of the lake or piped away. It can be used to heat many buildings, as a kind of District Heating, or to generate electricity. It costs only a third as much as oil heating.

High-temperature collectors

These are sophisticated pieces of equipment that can move to catch the maximum rays from the sun. They are also able to focus the rays on material that absorbs their heat. They can generate electricity and high temperatures for industrial processes. When they are built on a large scale, they are called solar furnaces – there is a solar furnace in the French Pyrenees that can produce temperatures of over 3,000 °C.

In northern Europe, northern America and other countries with long, cold winters, the sun's heat must be captured in summer so that it can be stored for the winter. Stones and bricks are used for this, just as they are in electric storage-heaters, but on a much bigger scale. They take up too much space in an ordinary house, but high-temperature collectors can heat factories, office blocks and other large buildings. This is done in Sweden.

Solar electricity

This can be generated by a solar furnace or by solar cells. Solar furnaces must be in an area where there is plenty of sunshine. Some furnaces have a lot of solar collectors, which heat a liquid that carries the heat to a central point. Others use reflectors to focus the energy on a central point.

Solar furnaces take up a lot of space and are expensive, but they are used in Japan, and the American states of California and Arizona.

Solar cells are used a lot in calculators. They work by means of a piece of silicon treated with chemicals that creates an electric current when light shines on it. The power can be increased by focusing light from a large area on to the cell.

Solar cells were originally developed for satellites. Today they are used in remote areas for telecommunications, irrigation and water pumps. They are too expensive to compete with mains electricity in areas which have it, but their cost is coming down.

Ocean heat

This form of solar power is similar to solar ponds. Four-fifths of the Earth's surface is covered with ocean. This means the ocean receives most of the sun's rays. The top 10 feet (3 metres) of the ocean surface contains more heat energy than the air surrounding the Earth. Beneath this, the temperature gets colder and colder. In tropical seas the difference in temperature between the upper and lower layers is at least 20 °C all year round, and this can be used to generate power.

The process is called Ocean Thermal Energy Conversion (OTEC). It works by the warm surface water heating a liquid in a tube to form a vapour. The vapour turns a turbine that drives an electrical generator, and electricity is carried to shore by cables. The vapour is cooled back to liquid by the deeper, colder water, and then the whole process starts again.

Although OTEC can only be used in tropical waters, it can work all year round and it could produce huge amounts of power. At the moment it's only in the experimental stages. Before it's developed further, scientists must investigate what changing the oceans' warm and cool areas would do to their ecology.

• Water power

The simplest form of water power is the water-mill. These have been known in Britain since Roman times. A water-mill works by the damming of a stream above the mill. The water then cascades down on to the paddles of the wheel and forces it to turn. The wheel drives machinery inside the mill, to grind corn, for example. Water-mills are still used in many parts of the world.

Hydroelectricity

Hydroelectricity is a more sophisticated kind of water power. It's clean, efficient and produces 6.7 per cent of the world's energy. Modern water-wheels, called water turbines, are a ring of curved blades. They are turned by fast-flowing water so that they drive generators.

The amount of power the water turbines produce depends on the amount of water, the force with which it flows, and the distance it falls. Because of this, it's used a lot in countries with mountains and fast-flowing streams, such as Switzerland, Canada, Sweden and Scotland.

Hydroelectricity produces energy that is cheap and constantly available. It has several disadvantages though. One is that building the stations is expensive. Another is that dams are usually needed, so much land is flooded. This means that the local ecology is damaged and people often have to leave their homes. A third disadvantage is that silt can build up to make the station unusable. Careful planning can lessen the damage to the environment – for example, fish ladders make it possible for fish to move upstream and down.

Wave power

The power in the movement of waves has interested scientists since the eighteenth century. In the last 20 years, Britain and Norway have tried to turn this movement into electricity.

Scientists think that for every metre a wave rises or falls in mid-ocean, 100 kilowatts of electricity could be generated. Nearer to the shore, it would be about 15 kilowatts – enough to power five large electric fires.

One way that researchers have tried to produce electricity is by an oscillating water column. This is a kind of cylinder, open at the base, that contains a column of water and an air space. The waves make the water column move upwards. As it moves it acts like a piston, squeezing the air through valves, and this air drives a turbine and generator. As the water falls again, air is sucked back into the cylinder. This system is being tested in Norway and Japan.

The Norwegians are also testing a wave buoy. This is a bell-shaped object that contains air and a turbo-generator. A central shaft runs through the buoy to the sea-bed. Waves make the buoy move up and down the shaft, forcing air to turn the turbo-generator.

British scientists are working on a device called a clam. This is made of a lot of bags of air linked together. Waves make the air rise and turn a turbine. As the waves fall, air is sucked back into the bags again.

One of the advantages of wave power is that the waves are most powerful in winter when most energy is needed. At one time, people were afraid that the devices would damage coastlines, but now it's believed they won't. Norway can now produce electricity from wave power at the same cost as conventional electricity.

A disadvantage is that the installations have to be extremely strong to stand up to storms. Another problem is

ALTERNATIVE ENERGY SOURCES

that salt water is very corrosive. In addition, they may be harmful to fish, but so far nobody can be sure of this.

Tidal power

France, China and the Soviet Union already have tidal power stations and Canada, Australia, India and Britain are interested in them. Tidal power stations need a barrier or barrage across bays and estuaries that have a big difference between high and low tides. The barrages contain turbines that are turned by the movement of the tides.

Tidal barrages were built in Europe as long ago as Norman times. They let in the rising tide and then trapped its water. This was used to drive water-wheels that were mostly of the 'undershot' kind, where the water runs under the wheel. These water-wheels provided power for grinding corn, for working bellows in iron-making furnaces and for machinery that sharpened knives, swords, scythes and so on. People stopped using them when steam power was invented in the nineteenth century.

The advantages of tidal power are that it is clean and renewable. It has several disadvantages. The installations are very expensive to build. Environmentalists are very worried that the barrages may alter the movement of the tides, which would affect wetlands around the estuaries. These wetlands are the habitat of much wildlife, especially wading and migrating birds. There are very few of these birds left, so their survival is very important. People are also concerned that tidal barrages would affect coastal sediments and the way that sewage is dispersed in the sea.

• Wind power

Winds are created by the air being unevenly heated by the sun. Warm air rises, cool air flows in to take its place, and a wind is created. Windmills have been used for over a thousand years and you can still see them in many parts of the world. The wind drives the sails, which drive machinery inside the mill.

Modern windmills are called wind turbines. Wind speeds increase above the ground, so the blades are placed high up on poles or towers. Inside the towers are generators. Some wind turbines have blades as long as 196 feet (60 metres). The blades can be turned to face the wind or turned away if the wind is too strong for them. Some of these modern wind turbines are controlled by computers.

Many communities in the United States share wind turbines – there are 15,000 in California alone. In Denmark people are encouraged to build their own windmills.

Large wind turbines as high as 492 feet (150 metres) can be grouped together to make wind farms. You can see these in Hawaii, Denmark, Scotland and Sweden.

Scientists made a study of wind farms for the European Community and suggested 400,000 sites for large-scale wind generation. Between them, these sites could produce three times the amount of electricity that the Community uses.

In July 1989, the Central Electricity Generating Board announced Britain's first wind farm. Twenty-five wind turbines will be built on 1 square mile (2.5 square kilometres) of land at Capel Cynon, west Wales. The wind farm will supply 5,000 houses with electricity. If this experiment works, wind farms will probably be built in the Pennines and Cornwall. Meanwhile research into off-shore wind turbines is under way in Norfolk and Suffolk.

Wind power is clean and renewable, and it is strongest in winter weather when most power is needed. The turbines can be built quickly in a range of sizes to suit everyone's needs. The disadvantages are that the small turbines need back-up systems when the wind is light and the large ones are very noisy. The large ones are often in remote areas, which means that they may spoil beautiful landscapes. When you compare this with the problems caused by the non-renewable sources of energy, it may be a small price to pay.

• Geothermal power

The surface of the Earth is cool, but its centre is made of hot, molten rock. When a volcano erupts it hurls this rock, which we call lava, out into the air. In some parts of the world, the Earth's surface has cracks in the rock that allow water to trickle through. The heat below the surface forces the water to rise as steam until it reaches the surface, where the drop in temperature turns it back into hot water. Sometimes the pressure forces the water high into the air, and this is known as a geyser.

In many countries people use the hot water or steam to heat buildings and water and to make electricity. Iceland is famous for its hot springs, which provide heat for two-thirds of the country's houses. They also heat vast greenhouses, and this cold northern country is able to export fruit and vegetables that are usually seen only in hot countries. Italy, the United States, the Soviet Union, New Zealand, Japan, Mexico, Kenya and the Philippines also use this type of heating.

Yet we are not limited to the hot water that rises naturally to the surface. It is possible to drill into the Earth and bring it up, or to break up rocks deep in the Earth and pump water over them to heat it. Right now, 50 countries are researching or using geothermal power.

Its advantages are that it is cheaper than conventional power and it could supply energy for thousands of years. Unfortunately, it's not completely clean. Some sites produce gas or liquid wastes, including carbon dioxide and hydrogen sulphide, and poisons such as mercury and arsenic. Another disadvantage is that removing underground rock could cause subsidence or even earth tremors. Also, no one knows what might be the long-term result of removing the heat from the Earth's core.

• Biomass power

'Biomass' is how scientists describe all living things and the products that can be made from them – for example, vegetable oils and cattle manure. There are not many figures for biomass power, because most of it is used in the less-developed countries and nobody keeps check on it. There are several different ways of producing it.

Animal power

For thousands of years, horses, donkeys, camels and oxen have been used to carry people and their goods and to pull loads. They are also used for ploughing and harrowing, turning wheels to pump water for irrigation and many other agricultural tasks.

In medieval England, people put dogs in wheels (like larger versions of the ones you see in hamster cages) to turn the spits on which meat was roasted. In the Arctic, dogs were used to pull sleighs, and in some parts of the world dogs and goats pull carts.

In central London, the big brewery companies still use shire-horses to pull their drays. They are more economical and easier to manage in crowded city streets. What's more, they probably don't get parking tickets!

The grazing animals (horses, oxen, camels, donkeys and goats) not only provide power, they also produce manure. This can be spread on the land to improve the soil and give good harvests.

ALTERNATIVE ENERGY SOURCES

On farms where livestock is farmed intensively, the manure is often 'digested' (broken down by the action of bacteria) to form carbon dioxide and methane. This is known as biogas, and it has about two-thirds of the energy of natural gas. If the carbon dioxide is removed from it, leaving pure methane, it is very similar to natural gas (which is 95 per cent methane). It can then be used as a form of power. Rotting plants and human waste in the form of sewage can be dealt with in a similar way to produce usable gas.

Burning

Dry forms of biomass are burnt to provide heat. Wood is used most often, but straw and rubbish can be burnt too.

At one time wood was the main source of energy for most people. Even today, it is still relied upon by 2.5 billion people – mainly in the less-developed countries, but also in the forested areas of the United States and Canada.

As we've seen, the main problem with wood is that if people cannot replace the trees as fast as they burn them, areas become deforested. This means the soil becomes poor and eroded. Burning wood also gives off carbon dioxide, which adds to the greenhouse effect. But if more trees were grown than burnt, there would be no increase because growing trees absorb carbon dioxide.

Straw-burning stoves are being used more and more in Europe to heat houses and to dry grain. Again, straw-burning gives off carbon dioxide, and it also means there is not enough straw left to provide bedding for animals. Straw mixed with animal manure makes excellent fertilizer for the soil, and so does straw ploughed directly back into the soil. So burning it takes away the supply of straw that is very useful to farmers.

Rubbish can also be burnt for fuel. Because the developed countries produce massive amounts of rubbish that needs to be got rid of, there's certainly no shortage of it. There are several hundred schemes in Europe that burn rubbish for heat, usually in the form of District Heating.

Burning rubbish has the advantage of disposing of some of our tons of waste. It also enables glass and metals to be recovered for recycling. It has three disadvantages: it only gives a low level of energy; much of it may contain poisonous substances that could give off harmful gases when burnt; and it produces carbon dioxide.

Britain, the United States and some other countries are investigating ways of heating dry biomass without air, rather as charcoal is made from wood. They are also testing ways of heating it with gases and liquids. This could give gas and solid and liquid fuels.

Fermentation and vegetable oils

If you've ever helped your parents to make beer or wine, you will know that when a sugar solution is mixed with yeast it produces alcohol. Alcohol can be used as a fuel.

Sugar cane, sugar beet and fruits can be used with yeast to make ethyl alcohol (ethanol). Starchy plants – potatoes, wheat and maize, for example – can be treated so that their starch turns into sugar to be used in the same way. The sugary liquid is boiled, ethanol is given off as a gas and is allowed to cool back into a liquid. This is called distillation.

This process uses a lot of heat, so scientists are researching other ways of producing pure ethanol. At present, 1 tonne of sugar produces up to 114 gallons (520 litres) of alcohol. The solid sugar cane left behind can be used for animal feed.

In many countries this alcohol is mixed with petrol to provide fuel for cars. The mixture is called gasohol. In some countries cars run on alcohol alone. In Brazil, for example, two million vehicles run on alcohol made from sugar cane, and eight million run on gasohol. In the United States, many small farms run their vehicles on alcohol. Several other countries, including France and Finland, are hoping to use more of this kind of fuel.

Burning alcohol and gasohol gives off carbon dioxide, but it doesn't produce hydrocarbons, nitrous oxides and the other harmful gases that come from burning petrol.

Vegetable oils, such as peanut, soya, sunflower, rape and palm, can provide fuel too. They can power diesel engines and are used in Brazil and the Philippines. But the problem with using food plants for fuel is that it may leave less of the produce to eat.

I think that proper cycle lanes should be made because if you have to share the road with a bus it is no joke. You should see the amount of gap they leave, it is about one foot. It seems they want to shrink you for a laugh. If it would be possible for cycle lanes to be built I could cycle to school and I would love that.

Letter to Early Times *from Graham Collins, aged 8, from Oxford*

CHAPTER SIX

Transport

We have seen that 20 per cent of the United Kingdom's energy is used for transport. In the whole European Community, no less than 85 per cent of the transport energy is used by road transport.

The average car covers 13,000 miles (20,917 kilometres) a year. This means that each year the car produces 77 pounds (35 kilograms) of hydrocarbons, 1,045 pounds (475 kilograms) of carbon dioxide and 22 tonnes of nitrous oxides. If it's running on leaded petrol, it produces 7 ounces (200 grams) of lead too.

This gives you a picture of the damage that transport is causing to our environment. We could lessen the damage by making improvements in three areas – the source of energy we use for transport, the type of vehicles we drive and the way in which our transport is planned.

• Sources of energy

Oil

Nearly all our transport energy comes from oil. The advantages of oil are that even a small amount can provide a lot of energy, so a car can carry enough to take it long distances. It can be stored without damage. It ignites and burns easily and it's simple to adjust the supply to provide as much power as the vehicle needs. The problem is, there's only enough oil left for about another 50 years.

Electricity

Electricity provides about 1 per cent of the United Kingdom's transport energy. It's mostly used by electrified railways. Electricity that is produced by burning fossil fuels or by nuclear energy has the same environmental disadvantages as any other energy gained in the same way. If the electricity were produced by renewable resources, it would be an ecologically good way of powering railways. Even using the conventional kind of electricity, rail transport causes less environmental damage than road transport.

Electricity could also be used to power trams and trolley-buses in cities. These were used in our cities until the end of the 1950s – the last British tram ran in Sheffield in 1960. Sadly, they were abandoned because they got in the way of motor traffic.

The pressure group Transport 2000 says that bringing back the tram is one way of improving our cities. Many cities, including Manchester, Birmingham and Sheffield, do have plans to start running them again, although these days they are often called 'light railways'.

Some vehicles that run on electricity have batteries, for example, milk-floats. Their large, heavy batteries can be recharged, but they can only travel a short distance between charges. For example, a small car can only travel for about 50 miles (80 kilometres) before recharging.

This means that electrically powered vehicles are useful for short distances but not for long journeys. They are also rather slow. This makes them suitable as milk-floats and industrial trucks, but not much good as cars. Yet it's possible that if enough money were invested in development, an electrically powered car could be produced – as long ago as 1899, a Frenchman called Camille Jenatzy set a world land speed record of 65.79 m.p.h. in one! In 1989 the French car manufacturer Peugeot announced that it was introducing an electrically powered version of its 205 car model.

Steam

Over the years there have been a number of steam-powered vehicles. In 1769, Nicholas Cugnot invented a three-wheel steam carriage that travelled at 4 m.p.h. Over 130 years later, in 1906, the Stanley brothers built a steam car that could go faster than petrol-powered cars and it reached 127.6 m.p.h. on Daytona Beach! These steam cars burnt coal, but it might be possible to produce steam in a way that didn't cause so much pollution.

Hydrogen

Water is made of hydrogen and oxygen, and if you pass an electric current through it you can divide them up. It's also possible to do this in reverse – hydrogen can be made to join up with oxygen and produce water and electric current. This is done in a piece of equipment known as a fuel cell.

Hydrogen can also be burnt, and this gives energy and water. Water is the only waste product, so it is a clean fuel. Unfortunately, it can explode very easily. It is also very difficult to store – as a gas, it takes up a lot of space, and as a liquid it has to be stored at very low temperatures.

Biofuels

In Chapter five we looked at 'biofuels' – fuels that come from living things. A farmer in Hampshire was said to have run his car on chicken manure for many years! Alcohol and gasohol are now widely used to power cars in several countries. In California there are plans to phase out petrol-driven cars over the next 20 years. Instead, vehicles will run on biofuels and electricity.

• Putting a brake on pollution

Until we find a cleaner way of powering our cars, we can try to make sure they produce less pollution. Unleaded petrol and catalytic converters are two pollutant-reducing methods we looked at earlier.

In the United States, scientists have discovered a less polluting type of petrol. It costs slightly more, but it produces 9 per cent less carbon monoxide and 80 per cent fewer sulphur dioxides.

But there's a much cheaper and simpler way of reducing the pollution from cars – and that is to use them less! 74 per cent of all recorded journeys are of 5 miles (8 kilometres) or less. Many of these journeys could be done on foot or on a bicycle, if the roads were safer. In Denmark 40 per cent of journeys are done on bicycles. In Britain the figure is only 4 per cent. We often jump into our cars to nip down to the shops to get something. We don't stop to think that by the time we have searched for a parking-space, the journey might have been quicker by bike. Nor do we stop to think of the unnecessary pollution we are causing. Next time, stop and think before you ask your parents to give you a lift!

Another way of cutting pollution is to share cars more. If only two people share, the pollution is halved. Four people in a car means that there is only a quarter as much pollution. If you live near a route that commuters use to get into town, you will know that most cars travel with just the driver inside.

The way that people drive also affects pollution. The person who drives in a relaxed, easy-going way uses 20 per cent less fuel than the person who roars away at traffic-lights and puts the brakes on at the last minute. Driving faster than 55 m.p.h. increases the use of fuel dramatically.

Most British cars can travel about 30 miles (48 kilometres) on 1 gallon (4.5 litres) of petrol. American cars do less, having larger engines, on the same amount. But a car has been invented which can do 6,000 miles (9,654 kilometres) to the gallon! It can only travel at 15 m.p.h., but it shows that massive savings could be made if the technology could be developed. There are designs for more practical cars that could do up to 90 miles (145 kilometres) to the gallon in cities and up to 110 miles (193 kilometres) on the open road.

We won't solve the pollution problems caused by cars until we find a clean renewable fuel for them to run on. But in the mean time, saving as much fuel as possible will reduce the damage to our environment.

• Types of transport

Road transport doesn't only cause damage to our countryside and pollution. It kills. More people have died in road accidents in the last 40 years than were killed fighting in the Second World War.

Rail transport

Most people agree that we need some kind of rail transport to reduce pollution and make our cities more pleasant to live in. The fuels that power trains do cause pollution, of course – but railways can carry more people for less fuel, so they create much less pollution than road transport.

It is likely that more and more trains will be powered by electricity in future. If this is produced from 'clean' fuel, trains would not cause any pollution at all.

The trains of the future may be lighter and more streamlined in their shape. There may even be new steam trains. These would use energy more efficiently than today's diesel-powered trains and would probably be used for freight.

93

At the moment, engineers are trying to design 'floating' trains. These move along on a cushion of air like a hovercraft. This reduces friction, and that reduces the amount of energy needed to move the train.

Magnetic levitation works on the same principle. With this, the train is lifted into the air by the repulsion of two magnets, one on the train and one on the track. But most of the research into this is concentrating on faster speeds rather than saving fuel. There is also the problem that the magnetic fields may harm people's health.

Water transport

In many parts of Europe, freight travels by river and canal. In Britain we hardly use our waterways, although 1,500 miles (2,413 kilometres) of them are navigable. Yet water transport is more efficient than road transport, and only costs about a third as much.

Even though our old waterways are neglected, a new canal is being made in South Yorkshire to carry coal from a mine to a power station. Perhaps this may encourage more businesses to think about the possibility of sending their freight by water.

Most long-distance freight is carried by ships. There's an exciting development here – people have rediscovered wind power. A yacht can travel faster than a steam ship, and in the old days of the great sailing-ships, the tea-clippers travelled very fast indeed. The Japanese 3,000-tonne freight vessel *Shin Aitoku Mari* and Greenpeace's ship *Rainbow Warrior II* are just two of the ships that have recently been given sails as well as engines. When the winds are right, the sails can be used to save fuel.

Air travel

Air travel uses up massive amounts of energy – five times as much as rail travel. It creates pollution not only from its fuel, but also from its noise. It's fast and convenient if you need to travel a long distance, but it's certainly not environmentally friendly.

Solar power might be an answer to this. In 1981 a plane called *Solar Challenger* flew 163 miles (262 kilometres) and crossed the English Channel. It was powered by 16,000 solar cells fixed to its wings and tail. These drove a small electric motor that turned a propeller. The aircraft weighed only 205 pounds (93 kilograms) and flew at only 30 m.p.h. but it showed that solar-powered planes were possible. What's more, the *Solar Challenger* flew in silence except for a faint hum from the propeller. Unfortunately, an extra source of fuel would probably be needed for a larger and faster aircraft.

An airship is a form of air transport which is much more energy-efficient than a plane. Early airships were filled with hydrogen, and many of them exploded. Modern ones use helium, which is much safer. They are usually powered by fossil fuels, but burn far less than aeroplanes do. At the moment they are used only for short journeys, but they could be used for longer journeys for passengers and freight.

• Transport planning

Environmentalists say that if transport systems were properly planned, we could save energy, reduce pollution and make our cities pleasanter places to live in. Sensible planning would cut the number of cars and lorries on the roads, provide efficient and cheap public transport and put long-distance freight on to trains and barges.

If public transport were safe, reliable and cheap, more people would use it instead of a car. Transport 2000 is lobbying for more investment in public transport and the kind of co-ordinated rail and bus service that would make it an easy and sensible way to travel. If the roads were less choked with cars, more people would use bicycles. At the moment riding a bicycle in town is unpleasant and dangerous. We should provide more cycle routes, as many European countries do, so that cyclists can ride in safety. After all, their form of transport produces no pollution at all.

Freight could be moved by water or rail. Electrically powered vehicles could be used more in town. Industries could be encouraged to base themselves near water and rail routes.

Biking in the city (is not much fun)

mountain bikes are good for rugged, uneven terrain (like British roads!)

NOISY TRANSPORT COMPANY

potholes

old road-workings

A typical example of how we waste opportunities to send more freight by rail in this country is London's new Covent Garden Market. This was moved out of its site in central London to a larger one south of the Thames at Nine Elms. This is situated right by the railway-line to Waterloo Station, but there is no rail access. Instead there are massive lorry-parks.

Traffic calming

Many European cities are trying a kind of planning called

'traffic calming'. The idea is that traffic should not be allowed to dominate cities.

Roads are being made narrower instead of wider, especially at crossroads. Cycle lanes are being provided. Speed limits are being reduced and 'sleeping policemen' (bumps in the road) are being added to slow down the traffic. Other ways of slowing it include putting bends and traffic islands in the roads, and planting trees so that drivers can't see far ahead.

In Stockholm, Sweden, out-of-town traffic has to pay a heavy toll to enter the city. This discourages motorists from driving into town and provides money for the public-transport system. Bordeaux, in France, is experimenting with different zones to control the traffic.

Traffic calming reduces the traffic by making it harder for motorists to get around. As the traffic lessens, more and more people are happy to walk and cycle rather than use their cars.

It is good to know the public can change things to suit the environment.

Take CFCs and aerosol sprays. A year ago most sprays contained CFCs, now a lot fewer brands do.

You have got a voice which people take notice of. The greenhouse effect is slowly changing the world. Slowly the government is starting to do something about it.

Press for change. We want a green world when we are adults.

Now some of the other problems are sorted out, how about doing something to save the rain forests? Did you know that a new species of animal dies out every day thanks to their destruction?

Use your voice. How long does it take to ask your parents to stop buying goods made from rain-forest wood? Minutes at the most. Do something, and do it today!

Letter to Early Times *from Simon Blake, aged 12, from St Peter in Buckinghamshire*

CHAPTER SEVEN

What *YOU* Can Do to Help

You are just one of 6,000 million people who live on our Earth. So can your actions really make a difference to its future?

Remember — The world is in our hands!

The answer is yes, they certainly can. Because if you try to live in a way that will save the world rather than destroy it, you won't be alone. Your example will encourage your friends and family to do the same – and, of course, you can add some gentle persuasion! Then they will tell their friends and families about helping to care for the environment. It's a bit like throwing a pebble into a pool – the ripples spread further and further out from where the pebble drops.

Ordinary people *can* make a difference. In 1972 Friends of the Earth organized a campaign to stop people from buying tiger, cheetah and leopard furs. In the end, these furs

99

were banned altogether. By forming a campaign group, the people of Luxulyan, Cornwall, prevented the Central Electricity Generating Board from building a nuclear power station near by. At Billingham, Cleveland, the residents stopped a disused salt-mine being turned into a nuclear-waste dump. In 1989, ships tried to unload toxic waste in Canada. The Canadian people simply refused to allow it and the ships had to set sail again with their dangerous cargo still on board.

You may not have the chance to achieve such major victories as these. Yet you can still have an effect on the environment by making small choices every day about how you should act.

Here are some ways in which you, your friends and your family can begin trying to save the Earth right now.

1. *Try not to waste energy*

Don't turn the heating up on a cold day so that you can wear thin clothes inside the house – put an extra sweater on instead. If you have central heating, turn off the radiators in empty rooms. Switch off the lights in empty rooms too. Do you leave the television and stereo on when nobody is watching or listening? Reach for the off switch again!

If you help with the cooking, don't waste gas or electricity. Try not to put a single dish in the oven – use the hob instead if possible. On the other hand, if there are two or three dishes that could go in the oven, don't use two or three rings at once.

If your cooker is electric, you can turn off the rings and the oven a few minutes before the food is cooked. Use a pan that fits the ring. If you are cooking vegetables, use only as much water as you really need. The same goes for kettles – don't fill yours up just to make one cup of tea. It's easier to judge the amount of water you need in the new jug-type kettles.

When you wash your hands, put the plug in the basin instead of letting the water run away all the time. If you have a shower, use it – it will take less hot water than a bath. If you only have a bath, don't fill it to the brim!

If you have a washing-machine and dishwasher, don't turn them on until they are full. Running them half-empty is a great waste of energy. Don't stand with the fridge door open while you wonder what to eat – make your mind up before you open the door. The fridge warms up when the door is open and it takes extra energy to make it cold again.

If there's a choice between a manual tool and an electric one, you know by now which one to go for. For example, cutting the lawn with a manual mower rather than an electric one saves a lot of energy. It also keeps you fit!

2. *Keep yourself informed about environmental issues*

The more you know about the problems, the more you can do to help solve them. Read the newspapers (including *Early Times!*) and 'green' magazines. Switch on the radio and television when there's a programme on the environment.

Find out what's happening in your neighbourhood. Is there a wildlife habitat near you that is threatened by development? Is there a factory that is causing pollution? Make your voice heard by joining local pressure groups.

3. *Before you throw anything away, stop and think. Might someone else have a use for it?*

Charities are often pleased to have old stamps, silver paper, milk-bottle tops, toys, books, magazines and old clothes. Re-use paper and polythene bags and plastic carrier bags. When you go shopping, take a carrier bag with you. When the bags are too tatty to hold the shopping, use them for putting rubbish in so that it stays neatly in the dustbin instead of spilling out to create litter.

101

Farm shops and wholefood shops are often pleased to have egg boxes back. Don't throw used envelopes away – send them off a second time with a sticker to explain that this is to save trees. You can buy these stickers in most wholefood shops – and, of course, they are made from recycled paper!

If you have a garden but no compost heap, start one. It's an excellent way of recycling potato peelings, apple cores, tea leaves – all the vegetable rubbish that comes from the kitchen. A good compost heap is also the first step towards successful gardening without chemicals because you can use it to fertilize the soil.

4. *Take as much rubbish as you can to local recycling centres*

There's a bottle bank in most towns these days. Save up all your jars and bottles and take them to it. Take off the tops first and *don't* leave the bag or box you took them in as litter!

You can probably find someone who will take your newspapers for recycling. Try the local council first. If they don't want them, ask around – there may be a local conservation group which will be glad to help. If you are stuck, ask Friends of the Earth (their address is on page 115).

Some councils also recycle plastic and aluminium – and some will actually pay you for aluminium cans! You can expect to get about 30p for 50 cans. This doesn't sound a lot, but we use over 2,000 million aluminium drinks cans each year. This works out to about £20,000,000 for the people who are smart enough to return them!

There are over 250 centres to take your cans to. They will give you re-usable bags to collect them in and a magnetic tester so you can be sure which ones are aluminium. You'll find the address for the Aluminium Can Recycling Association on page 117.

5. *If you have a choice, avoid buying packaged goods*

If the goods you want are on the counter both packaged and unpackaged, choose the unpackaged ones. You may find that the storekeeper will try to wrap them up just as much, but say that you don't want the extra wrapping and explain politely why not. If you think that something has got far too much packaging, you can complain to the Packaging Council (address on page 119).

6. *Don't waste paper*

Don't use throwaway paper products such as tissues, kitchen paper and napkins – ask your parents to buy cotton ones instead. When you are writing, use both sides of the paper. If you have any paper that has already been used on one side, it will do for rough paper.

7. *Buy recycled paper products*

Toilet paper made from recycled paper is now on sale in wholefood shops and many supermarkets, so persuade your parents that it's a good idea to buy it. You can probably find attractive stationery, exercise books and greetings cards too. If you can't, you'll find some addresses on page 118 and 120 that will help you.

8. *Before you buy anything, ask yourself if you really need it*

You don't need everything advertisements say you do – nor do you need everything that your friends have! Try to avoid buying things you really don't have any use for. It will save you money and avoid more waste.

9. *Persuade your parents not to buy detergents based on phosphates*

Most detergents, such as soap powder and washing-up liquids, have phosphates in them. When they get into our river systems, they cause a process called 'eutrophication'. This means that they provide nutrients for tiny water plants. It makes them grow so much that they smother bigger water plants and kill them, so that there is less food and shelter for wildlife. Most shops now sell detergents that have no phosphates in them.

10. *Walk or cycle whenever possible*

Stop and think before you ask your parents to get out the car. Could you walk instead? If it's too far to walk, could you ride your bicycle? If not, could you use public transport? If it's dark or the roads are dangerous, your parents will probably want to drive you. In this case, see if you can share the journey with someone else.

11. *Join local campaigns for cycle lanes*

Cycling would be safer for everyone if there were more cycle lanes – and if cycling were safer, more people would get on their bikes and leave their cars at home.

12. *Use the facilities in your own area whenever you can*

Don't go across town to shops, youth clubs, sports centres and so on if there are some in your area. Crossing town means using transport and that means pollution.

13. *Never drop litter*

If you are taking drinks or food out with you, make sure

you have a bag to put the containers in until you can find a rubbish-bin. If you can't find a bin, bring them home. If your friends drop litter, try to persuade them to pick it up and take it home. If they won't, do it yourself – and don't take any notice if they laugh at you. Clear up the litter outside your home and school.

Why not organize a 'clean-up day' with your friends to clear all the litter in the local park or any place where litter is a problem? If you can get the local newspaper to give you some publicity, this is twice as good. The litter will be cleared and people will read about it. Maybe they will ask themselves why they drop litter for other people to clear up!

14. *When you visit the country, remember the Country Code*

THE COUNTRY CODE

- Guard against risk of fire
- Fasten all gates securely
- Keep dogs under proper control
- Keep to paths across farmland
- Avoid damaging fences, hedges and walls
- Leave no litter
- Safeguard water supplies
- Go carefully on country roads
- Respect the life of the countryside
- Protect wild life, wild plants and trees

It's easy for people who live in towns to think of the countryside as a sort of recreation park. They forget that people live and work there. If their dog chases cows or sheep, they sometimes say, 'Oh, he's only playing with them. He won't bite.' They don't realize that frightened cows give less milk and frightened sheep lose their lambs. They have never seen a sheep that has been savaged by a dog and they think the farmer is being unreasonable if he threatens to shoot their dog.

You have probably seen advertisements where a family drives the car into a cornfield and has a picnic. Don't do it. Each stalk of grain is part of the farmer's income, who will be rightly annoyed if people trample them down. And don't swing on gates or climb walls and fences – someone has to repair them as they gradually give way under people's weight.

Gates in the countryside are sometimes heavy and difficult to shut. You may be tempted to leave them. Again, don't do it. Do you want to be responsible for a cow or sheep escaping and being injured or killed by a car? You wouldn't go out and leave your front door open, so don't leave gates open either.

Don't think it's all right to drop litter in a hedge where it's hidden. Cows have a habit of eating polythene bags, and that can kill them. Cans and bottles can cut an inquisitive animal.

Respect 'No Parking' signs – there's usually a good reason for them. If you are camping, don't dig toilet holes or use detergents near a stream. Our countryside is already under threat, so make sure your visit leaves no scars upon it.

15. *Avoid using products containing CFCs*

Don't buy any aerosol products unless you are sure that they don't contain CFCs or other ozone-layer damaging chemicals. Many are labelled, but if you are in doubt, you can get a list of 'safe' products from Friends of the Earth. Many products now use pump action instead, and you can usually find other options – for example, you can buy a roll-on or stick deodorant instead of an aerosol one.

16. *Don't buy tropical hardwoods*

Persuade your parents not to buy household goods made of tropical hardwoods. You don't really need a mahogany lavatory seat rather than a pine one – it might look nice, but so do the rain forests. More important, they are vital to the future of the Earth. If you are buying wooden items – toys, pencil boxes and so on – try to find out what wood they are made of. Hardwood products are usually more expensive than pine, and the wood usually has a finer grain. If you are in doubt, don't buy.

17. *Don't buy anything that involves cruelty to animals*

If you buy cosmetics, choose those that haven't been tested on animals. Beauty Without Cruelty and Body Shop are names to look for. Don't buy perfumes or pet foods that use whale products.

Persuade your parents to buy free-range eggs and chickens – you can get them in most supermarkets. Some butchers now stock meat from humanely farmed cows, pigs and sheep too. If your parents think it's too expensive, suggest that the family eats vegetarian meals some days to make it more affordable.

Don't buy anything made of animal fur. If you hear someone saying they want a fur coat, tell them about the cruelty of trapping. Remind them that some people will look at them with horror rather than admiration when they wear it.

18. *Join conservation organizations*

You'll find a list in Chapter eight. Support them with an annual subscription and help with fund-raising. You can do this by joining in sponsored runs, car-boot sales, jumble sales and so on. You'll meet lots of people who feel the same way as you do. At the same time, you'll be helping the Earth to survive.

19. *Help to clean up your local environment*

There's probably a group in your area which spends weekends cleaning up ponds, streams and woodland. Take some friends along and join in – you'll have fun as well as helping the environment. Your local library will probably know of such a group. If not, contact the British Trust for Conservation Volunteers (address on page 114).

any help appreciated

20. *Use your consumer power*

Try to buy only goods that are environmentally friendly. You can sometimes recognize these by reading the labels carefully. An easier way is to check in books such as *The Green Consumer Guide* and *The Green Consumers' Supermarket Shopping Guide*. They aren't infallible, but they are a help.

21. *Protest about things you feel strongly about*

Don't hesitate to make formal protests. You can report local pollution to environmental health offices. If it concerns a beach, write to the Marine Conservation Society. You can also write to the companies that are responsible for the pollution.

If developers are planning buildings you object to, write to the Planning Officer at your local council and to local councillors (you'll find their names and addresses at your library). If you can get a group of protesters together, you may be able to get publicity in the local newspaper. You can also write to your MP.

If your town doesn't have bottle banks or recycling centres, write to your local councillors and ask for them. Start a campaign to encourage other people to do the same.

22. *Try to ensure that household rubbish is disposed of in the right way*

Old refrigerators, cookers and so on should be taken to the local authority dump. If your parents haven't got transport, the council will organize collection. (But first make sure that no local charity wants them.) Put old car oil in cans and take it to the local authority dump – you'll find special facilities there for dealing with it. Don't burn old tyres and furniture – they often give off poisonous fumes. Take them to the dump too.

23. *Buy organic products wherever possible*

Try to persuade your parents that organic food is best. It's more expensive, and not always easy to find, but food grown with chemicals just isn't good for you. If more and more people want organic food, the farmers will grow it for them. This means fewer chemicals will be sprayed on our countryside and that our diet will be healthier too.

24. *Try to reduce noise pollution*

We live in a very noisy world. There's the noise of traffic, machinery and aircraft. Then there's the extra noise of televisions, radios and Muzak. Don't add to it. If you have the window open, turn your radio, stereo or television

down. Don't take your radio outside – other people may not want to hear it. Playing your radio in the countryside is pollution, just as litter is. If you've grown up in a noisy society, you might find it difficult at first just to listen to trees rustling or waves breaking. Try it. It's the natural noise of our Earth you can hear.

25. *Make a nature reserve in your garden*

If you have a garden, make sure there's a place for wild creatures in it. This means leaving a part of it wild and untidy. Untouched hedge bottoms and piles of leaves make winter homes for many animals. (Never burn leaves without checking first that there isn't a hedgehog asleep in them.) Don't use chemicals. Slug pellets will poison slugs, but they will also poison the birds and hedgehogs that eat them. Insecticides will kill aphids, but they will also kill the ladybirds that eat them. A book on organic gardening will give you better methods of dealing with garden pests.

Wildlife will be attracted by certain plants. Here's a list:
Butterflies: buddleias, sedums, Michaelmas daisies, sweet-williams and flowering herbs.

your garden as a nature reserve...

Bees: flowering herbs, lavender, foxgloves and many other flowers. They also love the flowering heads of leeks gone to seed.

Ground beetles: these will eat many insect pests. They like ground-hugging plants such as horizontal cotoneaster, hypericum and creeping dead nettles.

Hoverflies: another useful predator. Plant French marigolds, dwarf convolvulus and poached egg plants to attract them.

Birds: almost any plant with berries will attract birds. They also like cover for nesting, such as hedges, ivy, evergreen bushes and trees.

All kinds of wildlife need water to drink and bathe in. If you put a dish of water out, you'll soon see how popular it is and you'll love watching the birds taking a dip. If you're lucky enough to have a pond, make sure there is one side that slopes gently. If not, put a little ramp in it. Some small creatures fall into ponds and cannot get out again if all the sides are steep.

If you don't have a pond, you can put earth in the bottom of an old washing-up bowl and add plants and stones. This will attract frogs, which will be able to spend the winter there without freezing.

Keep the water clean and free from algae. If you just have a dish, this means scrubbing it out. If you have a pond, there are plants that will keep the algae away. You should be able to get these from a garden centre, or from a pet shop that sells aquariums.

Keep the water free from ice in the winter. Break the ice on cold days and add a little warm water (not hot) to stop it freezing again for a while. Many animals die from thirst in hard winters.

If you don't have a garden, try to make a miniature wildlife reserve on a bit of waste ground. There may be some next to your house or the school playground.

26. *Put out food for wild creatures in winter*

You can buy special nut and seed mixtures for birds, but you can also feed them on household scraps. They will like bread, biscuits, cake, fat, meat, cooked potatoes and rice, cereal and so on. *Never* give them raw food that grows in bulk when it's moistened – it will swell in their stomachs and kill them. Blue tits will enjoy coconut halves hung from a branch. Some birds (and hedgehogs and foxes) will eat cat and dog food, and squirrels will raid nut containers. Put all food well out of the reach of cats.

Don't feed birds between April and November – the young birds cannot digest an artificial diet.

So there are 26 pointers towards saving the Earth. It won't always be easy to follow them. Your friends and family may not always agree with you, and sometimes you may desperately want to do something that's not 'green'. But some of them will become a habit, and there are some your parents are bound to like – saving energy, for instance, will keep the fuel bills down! And if you can manage to carry out at least some of them, you will know that you are contributing to saving the Earth. Right now, that's the most important cause there is.

CHAPTER EIGHT

'Green' Organizations

The British Trust for Conservation Volunteers
36 St Mary's Street
Wallingford
Oxon. OX10 0EU

British Trust for Ornithology
Beech Grove
Station Road
Tring
Herts. HP23 5NR

Campaign for Nuclear Disarmament
22–24 Underwood Street
London N1 7JG

Centre for Alternative Technology
Llwyngwern Quarry
Machynlleth
Powys
Wales SY20 9AZ

CLEAR (Campaign for Lead-Free Air)
3 Endsleigh Street
London WC1H 0DD

Conservation Trust
George Palmer Site
Northumberland Avenue
Reading
Berks. RG2 7PW

Consumers Against Nuclear Energy
P.O. Box 697
London NW1 8YQ

Council for Environmental Education
Department of Education
School of Educational Studies
University of Reading
London Road
Reading
Berks. RG1 5AQ

Council for the Protection of Rural England
Warwick House
25 Buckingham Palace Road
London SW1W 0PP

Friends of the Earth
26–28 Underwood Street
London N1 7JQ

The Green Alliance
60 Chandos Place
London WC2N 4HG

Green CND
23 Lower Street
Stroud
Glos. GL5 2HT

Greenpeace
30–31 Islington Green
London N1 8XE

Marine Conservation Society
9 Gloucester Road
Ross-on-Wye
Herefordshire HR9 5BU

National Society for Clean Air
136 North Street
Brighton
East Sussex BN1 1RG

The National Trust
36 Queen Anne's Gate
London SW1H 9AS

ENVIRONMENTALLY YOURS

Nature Conservancy Council
Northminster House
Northminster Road
Peterborough
Cambs. PE1 1UA

Population Concern
231 Tottenham Court Road
London W1P 9AE

Royal Society for Nature Conservation
The Green
Nettleham
Lincoln
Lincs. LN2 2NR

The Royal Society for the Protection of Birds and Young Ornithologists'
Club
The Lodge
Sandy
Beds. SG19 2DL

The Soil Association
86 Colston Street
Bristol
Avon BS1 5BB

The Tidy Britain Group
The Pier
Wigan WN3 4EX

Transport 2000
Walkden House
10 Melton Street
London NW1 2EJ

CHAPTER NINE

Useful Addresses

The Aluminium Can Recycling Association (for information about recycling)
I-Mex House
52 Blucher Street
Birmingham B1 1QU

The Aluminium Federation (for information about recycling)
Broadway House
Calthorpe Road
Birmingham B15 1TN

Animal Aid
7 Castle Street
Tonbridge
Kent TN9 1BH

Beauty Without Cruelty (for cosmetics without animal ingredients or testing)
37 Avebury Avenue
Tonbridge
Kent TN9 1TL

British Glass Manufacturers' Confederation (for information about recycling)
Northumberland Road
Sheffield S10 2UA

British Paper and Board Industry Federation (for information about recycling)
3 Plough Place
Fetter Place
London EC4

British Union for the Abolition of Vivisection
16A Crane Grove
Islington
London N7 8LB

British Waste Paper Association (for information about recycling)
Alexander House Business Centre
Station Road
Aldershot
Hants. GU11 1BQ

The Can Makers' Information Service (for information about recycling)
36 Grosvenor Gardens
London SW1

Chickens' Lib
P.O. Box 2
Holmfirth
Huddersfield HD7 1QT

Civic Trust
17 Carlton House Terrace
London SW1Y 5AW

Compassion in World Farming
20 Lavant Street
Petersfield
Hants. GU32 3EW

Conservation Papers (for recycled paper products)
228 London Road
Reading
Berks. RG6 1AH

Countryside Commission
John Dower House
Crescent Place
Cheltenham
Glos. GL50 3RA

Cyclists' Touring Club
69 Meadrow
Godalming
Surrey GU7 3HS

The Henry Doubleday Research Association
The National Centre for Organic Gardening
Ryton-on-Dunsmore
Coventry CV8 3LG

Institute of Trading Standards Administration
4/5 Hadleigh Business Centre
351 London Road
Hadleigh
Essex SS7 2BT

National Federation of City Farms
The Old Vicarage
66 Fraser Street
Windmill Hill
Bedminster
Bristol
Avon BS3 4LY

Neighbourhood Energy Action
2/4 Bigg Market
Newcastle-upon-Tyne NE1 1WW

Oxfam
274 Banbury Road
Oxford
Oxon. OX2 7DZ

Packaging Council
C/o INCPEN
College House
Great Peter Street
London SW1P 3NQ

Pedestrians' Association
1 Wandsworth Road
London SW8 2WX

Ramblers' Association
1 Wandsworth Road
London SW8 2WX

Royal Society for the Prevention of Cruelty to Animals
The Causeway
Horsham
West Sussex RH12 1HG

Save-a-Can (for information about recycling)
Elm House
19 Elmshott Lane
Cippenham
Nr Slough
Berks. SL1 5QS

Town and Country Planning Association
17 Carlton House Terrace
London SW1Y 5AS

Traidcraft plc (for Third World products, recycled paper goods, etc.)
Kingsway
Gateshead
Newcastle-upon-Tyne NE11 0NE

The Vegan Society
33–35 George Street
Oxford
Oxon. OX1 2AY

The Vegetarian Society
Parkdale
Dunham Road
Altrincham
Ches. WA14 4QG

The Woodland Trust
Autumn Park
Dysart Road
Grantham
Lincs. NG31 6LL

World Wide Fund for Nature (formerly the World Wildlife Fund)
Panda House
Weyside Park
Godalming
Surrey GU7 1XR

Index

THE EARLY BOOK OF CROSSWORDS

There are TV and radio puzzles, Hallowe'en puzzles, skeleton puzzles, science puzzles as well as straightforward crossword puzzles to keep you going for hours, days, weeks, months – in fact, as long as your brain can stand it. Whether you're a beginner or an addict, this book of crosswords from *The Early Times* will make you think and keep you puzzling.

CAN YOU GET WARTS FROM TOUCHING TOADS?

Doctor Pete Rowan

TV-AM's Doctor Pete answers questions that children ask him on every subject from warts to hiccups, to the speed at which a sneeze travels.

WORD PUZZLES

David Smith and Veronica Millington

An entertaining collection of puzzles covering a wide variety of areas of interest.

PUFFIN BOOK OF ROYAL LONDON

Scoular Anderson

Nowadays the word palace can mean any grand building, but this is a book about a very special group of palaces – the Royal Palaces of London – where the kings and queens of Britain lived and where the present Queen lives today.

Find out which were the favourite palaces and which one had a nasty pong; how the royals got about before cars, trains and buses; why they were sometimes sentenced to death and executed at the Tower; what they did for entertainment and what they ate at the royal banquets! Banquets, beefeaters and beheadings abound in this hilarious guide to Royal London.

WELL, WELL, WELL

Dr Peter Rowan

Find out what your body can (and can't) do; how its many parts work together to keep you healthy; what happens when things go wrong and who and what can make you better. Dr Pete gives some top tips on how to keep yourself fit, as well as some breath-taking facts which will amaze and amuse you.

ATTACKS OF OPINION

Terry Jones

Whether you agree or disagree with them, you can't ignore Terry Jones's satirical articles on topical and controversial issues, written in his own ironical, biting style, with brilliant cartoons by Gerald Scarfe.

THE ANIMAL QUIZ BOOK

Sally Kilroy

Why do crocodiles swallow stones? Which bird migrates the furthest? Can kangaroos swim? With over a million species, the animal kingdom provides a limitless source of fascinating questions. In this book Sally Kilroy has assembled a feast for enquiring minds – from domestic animals to dinosaurs, fish to footprints, reptiles to record breakers. Discover where creatures live, how they adapt to their conditions, the way they treat each other, the dangers they face – you'll be surprised how much you didn't know.

EUROPE: UP AND AWAY

Sue Finnie

A lively book packed with information about Western Europe which includes sections on stamps, car numbers and languages as well as topics related to an individual country (from Flamenco dancing to frogs' legs).

THE SECOND PUFFIN CROSSWORD PUZZLE BOOK

Alan Cash

Another challenging crossword puzzle collection, including specialist puzzles for experts in science, literature and loads of other subjects. There are plenty of cryptic and general clues, too – enough to keep all crossword addicts happy.

Non-fiction from Dick King-Smith

COUNTRY WATCH

Animal watching can be fascinating and fun – if you know what to look out for and how best to observe it. There are so many different kinds of animals to see in the British countryside and it's not only the unusual ones that are interesting. *Country Watch* is full of surprising facts (did you know that the tiny mole can burrow its way through thirty pounds of earth in an hour?) and Dick King-Smith has lots of marvellous stories to tell about his own encounters with animals over the years.

TOWN WATCH

It's surprising how many wild animals there are to be seen in towns today. *Town Watch* is crammed with information about the many mammals, birds, insects and reptiles that live within the bounds of our towns and cities. Did you know that the cheeky house-sparrow is really one of the tough guys of the bird world, roaming the city in gangster-style mobs? From rubbish-tip pests like rats and cockroaches to protected species such as owls and bats, this book has a wealth of information and stories about urban wildlife.

WATER WATCH

If you look at a map of the world, you'll see that most of its surface is sea. We are surrounded by water – all around us there are lakes, ponds, rivers and streams – not to mention man-made waterways like canals. On holiday at the seaside you can enjoy identifying all the different kinds of gull, or if you're near a rocky coastline you might even see a seal! And there are all sorts of water birds – some with very unusual habits – living near lakes and marshes. You'd have to be lucky to spot an otter but if you're patient and observant, there are some fascinating animals to be spotted in and around a garden or village pond.

GOING IT ALONE

Jody Tresidder

Ever thought it's time to leave home? Ever thought you'd like a flat of your own? And when the moment comes to choose, are you going to stick with school or college or go for a real job? Or could you go off abroad? Or even set up a company of your own? Here at last are the answers for every teenager who feels it's time they took control of their own lives.

WHOSE SIDE ARE YOU ON?

Martyn Forrester

Smoking – nuclear weapons – bullfighting – blood sports – all issues of tremendous importance, where you need to know the facts before you form your own opinions. This book has all the arguments in one book, presented by the people who really know what they are talking about: the supporters and opposers themselves.

GIRLS ARE POWERFUL

ed. Susan Hemmings

How does being a girl or a young woman affect the way people treat you? The way you are allowed to look and dress? Your friendships? And how are all these experiences affected by your class and race? *Girls are Powerful* looks at all these issues and more. But it's not a book 'just' for girls. The pieces in this collection are written by young women aged from seven to twenty-two, but they contain ideas which will open up discussions between women of all ages – perhaps for the first time.

CROSSWORD CRACKERS

Colin Gumbrell

A carefully thought-out, original and inventive collection of crosswords with clues covering a wide range of general knowledge.

MORE CROSSWORD CRACKERS

Colin Grumbrell

Nuts may be easier to crack than these crosswords, but they aren't half the fun! Three different sorts of crosswords ensure there's never a dull moment with the puzzles in this fascinating and original book. Whether you're a beginner or an experienced puzzler, you can be certain that there will be plenty to intrigue and delight you.

CODES FOR KIDS

Burton Albert jnr.

A fascinating collection of codes and cyphers. Confound your enemies! Confuse your friends!

CHECK OUT CHESS
Bob Wade and Ted Nottingham

The fun, easy way to learn to play chess. With this book you will easily acquire the sound basic skills necessary for success – many of the exercises have been especially developed by the authors and all tried and tested with beginners.

THE PUFFIN BOOK OF AMERICAN FOOTBALL
Simon Kilner

From tactics to the razzmatazz of the Super Bowl, from the origins of the sport to profiles of the NFL clubs, from college football to the game in Britain, this acclaimed introduction to one of television's most spectacular sport tells you almost everything you could wish to know about American football.

HOW TO SURVIVE
Brian Hildreth

If you ever go hiking, camping, climbing or canoeing – or even if you're just taking a plane or boat trip – this book should be part of your essential equipment. Written by the author of an air force survival handbook, it's an indispensable manual for anyone lost – or risking getting lost – in the great outdoors.